Credits

Footprint credits

Editorial: Nicola Gibbs
Maps: Kevin Feeney
Cover: Pepi Bluck

Publisher: Patrick Dawson
Managing Editor: Felicity Laughton
Advertising: Elizabeth Taylor
Sales and marketing: Kirsty Holmes

Photography credits
Front cover: Jerema/Dreamstime.com
Back cover: julian elliott/Shutterstock

Printed in Great Britain by CPI Antony Rowe,
Chippenham, Wiltshire

MIX
Paper from
responsible sources
FSC® C013604
www.fsc.org

Every effort has been made to ensure that the
facts in this guidebook are accurate. However,
travellers should still obtain advice from
consulates, airlines etc about travel and visa
requirements before travelling. The authors
and publishers cannot accept responsibility
for any loss, injury or inconvenience however
caused.

Contains Ordnance Survey data
© Crown copyright and database
right 2013

Publishing information

Footprint *Focus Dorset, New Forest
& Isle of Wight*
1st edition
© Footprint Handbooks Ltd
May 2013

ISBN: 978 1 909268 20 3
CIP DATA: A catalogue record for this book
is available from the British Library

® Footprint Handbooks and the Footprint
mark are a registered trademark of Footprint
Handbooks Ltd

Published by Footprint
6 Riverside Court
Lower Bristol Road
Bath BA2 3DZ, UK
T +44 (0)1225 469141
F +44 (0)1225 469461
footprinttravelguides.com

Distributed in the USA by Globe Pequot Press,
Guilford, Connecticut

The content of Footprint *Focus Dorset, New
Forest & Isle of Wight* has been updated from
Footprint's *England Handbook* which was
researched and written by Charlie
Godfrey-Faussett.

Contents

5 Introduction
   4 *Map: Dorset, New Forest and Isle of Wight*

6 Planning your trip
   6 Best time to visit England
   6 Transport in England
   9 Where to stay in England
   12 Food and drink in England
   13 Essentials A-Z

18 Dorset
   30 *Map: Lyme Regis to Exmouth*
   32 Listings

39 Salisbury and around
   39 *Map: Salisbury*
   46 Listings

49 Winchester and around
   50 *Map: Winchester*
   56 Listings

58 New Forest
   61 *Map: New Forest*
   63 Listings

66 Isle of Wight
   68 *Map: Isle of Wight*
   76 Listings

81 Footnotes
   82 Index

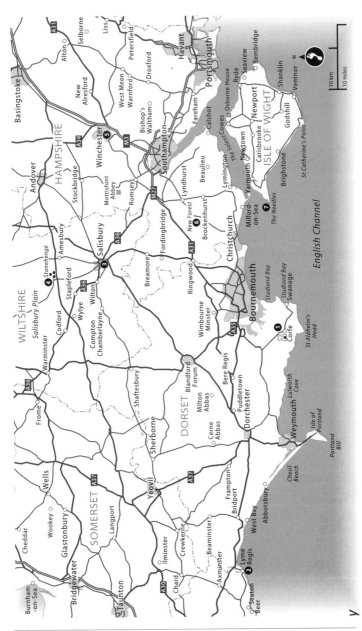

Congratulations: you have chosen to explore one of England's most naturally stunning and historically inspiring regions, encompasses ancient forests and cities, rural villages, sweeping beaches, hidden coves, charming islands, ancient manor houses, abbeys and hill forts.

Highlights include a UNESCO World Heritage Site, the Jurassic Coast – home to Britain's most important dinosaur finds and the wonderful Durdle Door, plus Victorian seaside towns such as Lyme Regis; Poole Harbour, second only in size to Sydney Harbour; and the Blue Flag beaches of Bournemouth and its vamped up neighbour Boscombe. There's nowhere quite like the New Forest. Contrary to its name, it's one of the few tracts of ancient forest left in Britain where deer still roam and visitors can enjoy a dazzling network of cycle tracks, footpaths, bridleways and pretty villages. The majestic cities of Salisbury and Winchester will transport you back to a gentler age of England with their impressive cathedrals and cosy tearooms. And then there's the ever mystical Stonehenge, where a new visitor centre is set to give you an even better insight into this 3000-year-old site. Sail across the Solent and the Isle of Wight has often been described as going back to an England of the 1950s where you can explore Queen Victoria's Osborne House or enjoy the prestigious Cowes Sailing Week, yet this quirky holiday island also attracts hip surfers and happening music festivals and serves some of the best ice cream in England.

Across the region is a growing awareness that visitors are demanding higher standards of accommodation, food and visitor experience, not to mention a firm eye on conservation, and we have sought to bring you our best recommendations for all. We hope you have a fabulous time exploring this vibrant region, and fingers crossed the sun shines for you, though in true British style there is plenty to explore under cover too.

Planning your trip

Best time to visit England

The weather in England is notoriously unpredictable. It is generally better between May and September, although it can be gloriously hot in April and cold and damp in August. The west of the country is milder and wetter than the east, whilst northern and mountainous areas are usually the coldest.

Transport in England

Compared to the rest of Western Europe, public transport in England is expensive and can be unreliable. Rail tickets, in particular, should be booked well in advance to avoid paying extortionate prices. Coach travel is cheaper but slower, and can be hampered by traffic problems in the big cities. If you plan to spend much time in rural areas, it may be worth hiring a car, especially if you are travelling as a couple or group. A useful website for all national public transport information is **Traveline** ① *T0871-200 2233, www.traveline.info.*

Air
England is a small country and air travel isn't necessary to get around. However, with traffic a problem around the cities, some of the cheap fares offered by budget airlines may be very attractive. There are good connections between London and all the regional airports, although travel from region to region without coming through London is more difficult and expensive. Bear in mind the time and money it will take you to get to the airport (including check-in times) when deciding whether flying is really going to be a better deal. The main airports serving Dorset and the south of England are Bournemouth, Southampton and Exeter. Dorset is also easily accessible from London Gatwick, London Heathrow and Bristol.

Airport information **Bournemouth International Airport** (BOH) ① *www.bournemouth airport.com*, is 4 miles northeast of the town. An airport shuttle bus, www.bournemouth-airport-shuttle.co.uk, runs daily 0700-1900 between the airport and the town centre and costs £5. A taxi into town costs approximately £20.

    Southampton Airport (SOU) ① *4 miles northeast, www.southamptonairport.com*, is well connected by bus into the centre. The Uni-Link bus, www.unilinkbus.co.uk, runs between the airport, university and centre every 15-20 minutes, taking around 40 minutes. A taxi to the centre costs approximately £17.

    Exeter International Airport (EXT) ① *5 miles east, www.exeter-airport.co.uk*, is just off the M5 motorway. **Stagecoach** service 56 runs a bus between the airport, train station and bus station. A taxi into town costs £15.

    Bristol International Airport (BRS) ① *T0870-121 2247, www.bristolairport.co.uk*, 8 miles south of the city centre, on the A38, has one terminal with standard facilities. A taxi to Bristol city centre costs £22, or the Bristol International Flyer coach links the airport with the railway station (Temple Meads) and the central bus station for onward connections, £11 return, 30 minutes.

Don't miss ...

1 **Corfe Castle and the nearby model village**, page 27.
2 **The Cob at Lyme Regis and fossil hunting along the Jurassic Coast**, page 31.
3 **The English Gothic architecture of Salisbury Cathedral**, page 42.
4 **Stonehenge and its new visitor centre**, page 43.
5 **The hospital of St Cross**, page 53.
6 **Cycling with a picnic in the New Forest**, page 58.
7 **A boat trip to see the Needles on the Isle of Wight**, page 75.

Numbers relate to the map on page 4.

Arriving in London National Express operates a frequent service between London's main airports. **London Heathrow Airport** ⓘ *16 miles west of London between junctions 3 and 4 on the M4, T0844-335 1801, www.heathrowairport.com,* is one of the world's busiest airports and has five terminals, so when leaving London, it's important to check which terminal to go to before setting out for the airport. To get into central London, the cheapest option is the London Underground Piccadilly Line (50 minutes). The fastest option is **Heathrow Express** ⓘ *T0845-6001515, www.heathrowexpress.com,* taking 15-20 minutes. There is a train service **Heathrow Connect** (T0845-748 4950, www.heathrowconnect.com), which takes 25 minutes. A taxi to central London takes one hour and costs £45-70.

  London Gatwick Airport ⓘ *28 miles south of London, off junction 9 on the M23, T0844-892 03222, www.gatwickairport.com,* has two terminals, North and South, with all the usual facilities. To central London, there is the **Gatwick Express** (T0845-850 1530, www.gatwick express.com), from £17.75 single online, which takes 30 minutes. **Thameslink** rail services run from King's Cross, Farringdon, Blackfriars and London Bridge stations. Contact **National Rail Enquiries** (T0845-748 4950, www.nationalrail.co.uk) for further information. **EasyBus** (www.easybus.co.uk) is the cheapest option, with prices starting at £9.99 for a single, taking just over an hour. A taxi takes a similar time and costs from around £60.

  London City Airport ⓘ *Royal Dock, 6 miles (15 mins' drive) east of the City of London, T020-7646 0000, www.londoncityairport.com.* Take the **Docklands Light Railway** (DLR) to Canning Town (seven minutes) for the **Jubilee** line or a connecting shuttle bus service. A taxi into central London will cost around £35.

  London Luton Airport ⓘ *30 miles north of central London, 2 miles off the M1 at junction 10, southeast of Luton, Beds, T01582-405100, www.london-luton.co.uk.* Regular **First Capital Connect** trains run to central London; a free shuttle bus service operates between the airport terminal and the station. **Green Line** (www.greenline.co.uk) coaches run to central London, as does **easyBus** (www.easybus.co.uk). A taxi takes 50 minutes, costing from £70.

  Stansted Airport ⓘ *35 miles northeast of London (near Cambridge) by junction 8 of the M11, T0844-335 1803, www.stanstedairport.com.* **Stansted Express** (T0845-600 7245, www.stanstedexpress.com) runs trains to London's Liverpool Street Station (45 minutes, £22.50 single). **EasyBus** (www.easybus.co.uk, from £2), **Terravision** (www.terravision.eu, £9) and **National Express** (www.nationalexpress.com, from £8.50) run to central London (55 minutes to East London, 1 hour 30 minutes to Victoria). A taxi to central London takes around an hour to 1 hour 30 minutes, depending on traffic, and costs around £99.

Rail

National Rail Enquiries ① *T08457-484950, www.nationalrail.co.uk*, are quick and courteous with information on rail services and fares but not always accurate, so double check. They can't book tickets but will provide you with the relevant telephone number. The website www.thetrainline.co.uk shows prices clearly.

Railcards There are a variety of railcards which give discounts on fares for certain groups. Cards are valid for one year and most are available from main stations. You need two passport photos and proof of age or status. A Young Person's Railcard is for those aged 16-25 or full-time students aged 26+ in the UK. Costs £28 for one year and gives 33% discount on most train tickets and some other services (www.16-25railcard.co.uk). A Senior Citizen's Railcard is for those aged over 60, is the same price and offers the same discounts as a Young Person's Railcard (www.senior-railcard.co.uk). A Disabled Person's Railcard costs £20 and gives 33% discount to a disabled person and one other. Pick up an application form from stations and send it to Disabled Person's Railcard Office, PO Box 11631, Laurencekirk AB30 9AA. It may take up to 10 working days to be delivered, so apply in advance (www.disabledpersons-railcard.co.uk). A Family & Friends Railcard costs £28 and gives 33% discount on most tickets for up to four adults travelling together, and 60% discount for up to four children. It's available to buy online as well as in most stations.

Road

Bus and coach Travelling by bus takes longer than the train but is much cheaper. Road links between cities and major towns in England are excellent, but far less frequent in more remote rural areas, and a number of companies offer express coach services day and night. The main operator is **National Express** ① *T08717-818178, www.national express.com*, which has a nationwide network with over 1000 destinations. Tickets can be bought at bus stations, from a huge number of agents throughout the country or online. Sample return fares if booked in advance: London to Manchester (4 hours 35 minutes) £28, London to Cambridge (2 hours 30 mins) £12. **Megabus** ① *T0900-160 0 900 (61p a min from BT landlines, calls from other networks may be higher), http://megabus.com*, is a cheaper alternative with a more limited service.

Full-time students, those aged under 25 or over 60 or those registered disabled, can buy a coach card for £10 which is valid for one year and gets you a 30% discount on all fares. Children normally travel for half price, but with a **Family Card** costing £16, two children travel free with two adults. Available to overseas passport holders, the **Brit Xplorer Pass** offers unlimited travel on all National Express buses. Passes cost from £79 for seven days, £139 for 14 days and £219 for its month-long **Rolling Stone Pass**. They can be bought from major airports and bus terminals.

Car Travelling with your own private transport is the ideal way to explore the country, particularly in areas with limited public transport. This allows you to cover a lot of ground in a short space of time and to reach remote places. The main disadvantages are rising fuel costs, parking and traffic congestion. The latter is particularly heavy on the M25 which encircles London, the M6 around Birmingham and the M62 around Manchester. The M4 and M5 motorways to the West Country can also become choked at weekends and bank holidays and the roads in Cornwall often resemble a glorified car park during the summer.

Motoring organizations can help with route planning, traffic advice, insurance and breakdown cover. The two main ones are: the **Automobile Association (AA)** ① *T0800-085 2721, emergency number T0800-887766, www.theaa.com*, which offers a year's breakdown cover starting at £38, and the **Royal Automobile Club (RAC)** ① *T0844-273 4341, emergency number T08000-828282, www.rac.co.uk*, which has a year's breakdown cover starting at £31.99. Both have cover for emergency assistance. You can still call the emergency numbers if you're not a member, but you'll have to a pay a large fee.

Vehicle hire
Car hire is expensive and the minimum you can expect to pay is around £100 per week for a small car. Always check and compare conditions, such as mileage limitations, excess payable in the case of an accident, etc. Small, local hire companies often offer better deals than the larger multinationals. Most companies prefer payment with a credit card – some insist on it – otherwise you'll have to leave a large deposit (£100 or more). You need to have had a full driver's licence for at least a year and to be aged between 21 (25 for some companies) and 70.

Bicycle
Cycling is a pleasant if slightly hazardous way to see the country. Although conditions for cyclists are improving, with a growing network of cycle lanes in cities, most other roads do not have designated cycle paths, and cyclists are not allowed on motorways. You can load your bike onto trains, though some restrictions apply during rush hour. See the website www.ctc.org.uk for information on routes, restrictions and facilities.

Where to stay in England

Accommodation can mean anything from being pampered to within an inch of your life in a country house spa hotel to glamping in a yurt. If you have the money, then the sky is very much the limit in terms of sheer splendour and excess. We have tried to give as broad a selection as possible to cater for all tastes and budgets, with a bias towards those that offer that little bit extra in terms of character.

If you can't find what you're after, or if someone else has beaten you to the draw, then the tourist information centres (TICs) will help find accommodation for you. Some offices charge a small fee (usually £1) for booking a room, while others ask you to pay a deposit of 10% which is deducted from your first night's bill. Details of town and city TICs are given throughout the guide.

Accommodation will be your greatest expense, particularly if you are travelling on your own. Single rooms are in short supply and many places are reluctant to let a double room to one person, even when they're not busy. Single rooms typically cost around 75% of the price of a double room, although some establishments do not charge single supplements.

Hotels, guesthouses and B&Bs
Area tourist boards publish accommodation lists that include campsites, hostels, self-catering accommodation, hotels, guesthouses and bed and breakfasts (B&Bs). Places participating in the VisitEngland system will have a plaque displayed outside which shows their grading, determined by a number of stars ranging from one to five. These

Price codes

Where to stay

££££	over £160	**£££**	£90-160
££	£50-90	**£**	under £50

Prices include taxes and service charge, but not meals. They are based on a one-night stay in a double room in high season.

Restaurants

£££	over £30	**££**	£15-30	**£**	under £15

Prices refer to the cost of a two-course meal for one person, without a drink.

reflect the level of facilities, as well as the quality of hospitality and service. However, do not assume that a B&B, guesthouse or hotel is no good because it is not listed by the tourist board. They simply don't want to pay to be included in the system, and some of them may offer better value.

Hotels At the top end of the scale there are some fabulously luxurious hotels, sometimes in beautiful locations. Some are converted mansions or castles, and offer a chance to enjoy a taste of aristocratic grandeur and style. At the lower end of the scale, there is often little to choose between cheaper hotels and guesthouses or B&Bs. The latter often offer higher standards of comfort and a more personal service, but many smaller hotels are really just guesthouses, and are often family run and every bit as friendly. Rooms in most mid-range to expensive hotels almost always have bathrooms en suite. Many upmarket hotels offer excellent room-only deals in the low season. An efficient last-minute hotel booking service is www.laterooms.com, which specializes in weekend breaks. Also note that many hotels offer cheaper rates for online booking through agencies such as www.lastminute.com.

Guesthouses Guesthouses are often large, converted family homes with up to five or six rooms. They tend to be slightly more expensive than B&Bs, charging between £30 and £50 per person per night, and though they are often less personal, usually provide better facilities, such as en suite bathroom, TV in each room, free Wi-Fi and private parking. Many guesthouses offer evening meals, though this may have to be requested in advance.

Bed and breakfasts (B&Bs) B&Bs usually provide the cheapest private accommodation. At the bottom end of the scale you can get a bedroom in a private house, a shared bathroom and a huge cooked breakfast from around £25 per person per night. Small B&Bs may only have one or two rooms to let, so it's important to book in advance during the summer season. More upmarket B&Bs, some in handsome period houses, have en suite bathrooms, free Wi-Fi and TVs in each room and usually charge from £35 per person per night.

Hostels

For those travelling on a tight budget, there is a network of hostels offering cheap accommodation in major cities, national parks and other areas of beauty, run by the Youth Hostel Association (YHA) ① *T01629-592600, or customer services T0800-019 1700,*

+44-1629-592700 *from outside the UK, www.yha.org.uk*. Membership costs from £14.35 a year and a bed in a dormitory costs from £15 to £25 a night. They offer bunk-bed accommodation in single-sex dormitories or smaller rooms, as well as family rooms, kitchen and laundry facilities. Though some rural hostels are still strict on discipline and impose a 2300 curfew, those in larger towns and cities tend to be more relaxed and doors are closed as late as 0200. Some larger hostels provide breakfasts for around £2.50 and three-course evening meals for £4-5. You should always phone ahead, as many hostels are closed during the day and phone numbers are listed in this guide. Advance booking is recommended at all times, particularly from May to September and on public holidays. Many hostels are closed during the winter. Youth hostel members are entitled to various discounts, including tourist attractions and travel. The YHA also offer budget self-catering bunkhouses with mostly dorm accommodation and some family rooms, which are in more rural locations. Camping barns, camping pods and camping are other options offered by the YHA; see the website for details.

Details of most independent hostels can be found in the *Independent Hostel Guide* (T01629-580427, www.independenthostelguide.co.uk). Independent hostels tend to be more laid-back, with fewer rules and no curfew, and no membership is required. They all have dorms, hot showers and self-catering kitchens, and some have family and double rooms. Some include continental breakfast, or offer cheap breakfasts.

Self-catering accommodation
There are lots of different types of accommodation to choose from, to suit all budgets, ranging from luxury lodges, castles and lighthouses to basic cottages. Expect to pay at least £200-400 per week for a two-bedroom cottage in the winter, rising to £400-1000 in the high season, or more if it's a particularly nice place. A good source of information on self-catering accommodation is the **VisitEngland** website, www.visitengland.com, and its *VisitEngland Self-catering 2013* guide, which lists many properties and is available to buy from any tourist office and many bookshops, but there are also dozens of excellent websites to browse. Amongst the best websites are: www.cottages4you.co.uk, www.ruralretreats.co.uk and www.ownersdirect.co.uk. If you want to tickle a trout or feed a pet lamb, **Farm Stay UK** (www.farmstay.co.uk) offers over a thousand good value rural places to stay around England, all clearly listed on a clickable map.

More interesting places to stay are offered by the **Landmark Trust** ① *T01628-825925, www.landmarktrust.org.uk*, who rent out renovated historic landmark buildings, from atmospheric castles to cottages, and the **National Trust** ① *T0844-800 2070, www.national trustcottages.co.uk*, who provide a wide variety of different accommodation on their estates. A reputable agent for self-catering cottages is **English Country Cottages** ① *T0845-268 0785, www.english-country-cottages.co.uk*.

Campsites
Campsites vary greatly in quality and level of facilities. Some sites are only open from April to October. See the following sites: www.pitchup.com; www.coolcamping.com, good for finding characterful sites that allow campfires; www.ukcampsite.co.uk, which is the most comprehensive service with thousands of sites, many with pictures and reviews from punters; and www.campingandcaravanningclub.co.uk. The **Forestry Commission** have campsites on their wooded estates, see www.campingintheforest.com.

Food and drink in England

Food

Only 30 years ago few would have thought to come to England for haute cuisine. Since the 1980s, though, the English have been determinedly shrugging off their reputation for over-boiled cabbage and watery beef. Now cookery shows such as *Masterchef* are the most popular on TV after the soaps, and thanks in part to the wave of celebrity chefs they have created, you can expect a generally high standard of competence in restaurant kitchens. Pub food has also been transformed in recent years, and now many of them offer ambitious lunchtime and supper menus in so-called gastro pubs.

Most parts of the country still boast regional specialities and thanks to the diversity of ethnic communities, restaurants offer food from all over the world. Enjoy Chinatowns and diverse styles of Asian cooking in the cities, or cosy up next to a roaring log fire to sample some more traditional country fare, such as or a ploughman's lunch with crumbly Blue Vinney cheese, or a Sunday roast with Yorkshire puddings. Afternoon Tea of jam and scones is ever popular, or indulge in some famous Dorset Apple Cake with a dollop of clotted cream. The south coast has a reputation for freshly caught fish, blue cheeses, specialist breads, local ales, handmade chocolates and locally made ice cream.

The biggest problem with eating out is the limited serving hours in some pubs and hotels, particularly in more remote locations. Some establishments only serve food 1200-1430 for lunch and 1830-2130 for supper. In small places especially, it can be difficult finding food outside these enforced times. Restaurants, fast-food outlets and the many chic bistros and café-bars, which can be found not only in the main cities but increasingly in smaller towns, often serve food all day till 2100 or later. The latter often offer very good value and above-average quality fare.

Drink

Drinking is a national hobby and sometimes a dangerous one at that. **Real ale** – flat, brown beer known as bitter, made with hops – is the national drink, but now struggles to maintain its market share in the face of fierce competition from continental lagers and alcopops. Many small independent breweries are still up and running though, as well as microbreweries attached to individual pubs, which produce far superior ales. In many pubs the basic ales are chilled under gas pressure like lagers, but the best ales, such as those from the independents, are 'real ales', still fermenting in the cask and served cool but not chilled (around 12°C) under natural pressure from a handpump, electric pump or air pressure fount. **Cider** (fermented apple juice) is also experiencing a resurgence of interest and is a speciality of Somerset. English **wine** is also proving surprisingly resilient: generally it compares favourably with German varieties and many vineyards now offer continental-style sampling sessions.

The **pub** is still traditional place to enjoy a drink: the best are usually freehouses (not tied to a brewery) and feature real log fires in winter, flower-filled gardens for the summer (even in cities occasionally) and most importantly, thriving local custom. Many also offer characterful accommodation and restaurants serving high-quality fare. Pubs are prey to the same market forces as any other business, though, and many a delightful local has succumbed to exorbitant property prices or to the bland makeover favoured by the large chains. In 2012, pubs were closing at the rate of 12 a week due to the recession.

Essentials A-Z

Accident and emergency

For police, fire brigade, ambulance and, in certain areas, mountain rescue or coastguard, T999 or T112.

Disabled travellers

Wheelchair users, and blind or partially sighted people are automatically given 34-50% discount on train fares, and those with other disabilities are eligible for the Disabled Person's Railcard, which costs £20 per year and gives a third off most tickets. If you will need assistance at a railway station, call the train company that manages the station you're starting your journey from 24 hrs in advance. Disabled UK residents can apply to their local councils for a concessionary bus pass. National Express have a helpline for disabled passengers, T08717-818179, to plan journeys and arrange assistance. They also sell a discount coach card for £10 for people with disabilities.

The English Tourist Board website, www.visitengland.com, has information on the National Accessible Scheme (NAS) logos to help disabled travellers find the right accommodation for their needs, as well as details of walks that are possible with wheelchairs and the Shopmobility scheme. Many local tourist offices offer accessibility details for their area.

Useful organizations include: **Radar**, T020-7250 3222, www.radar.org.uk. A good source of advice and information. It produces an annual National Key Scheme Guide and key for gaining access to over 9000 toilet facilities across the UK. **Tourism for all**, T0845-124 9971, www.holidaycare.org.uk, www.tourismforall.org.uk. An excellent source of information about travel and for identifying accessible accommodation in the UK.

Electricity

The current in Britain is 240V AC. Plugs have 3 square pins and adapters are widely available.

Health

For minor accidents go to the nearest casualty department or an Accident and Emergency (A&E) Unit at a hospital. For other enquiries phone NHS Direct 24 hrs (T0845-4647) or visit an NHS walk-in centre. See also individual town and city directories throughout the book for details of local medical services.

Money → *For up-to-date exchange rates, see www.xe.com.*

The British currency is the pound sterling (£), divided into 100 pence (p). Coins come in denominations of 1p, 2p, 5p, 10p, 20p, 50p, £1 and £2. Banknotes come in denominations of £5, £10, £20 and £50. The last of these is not widely used and may be difficult to change.

Banks and bureaux de change

Banks tend to offer similar exchange rates and are usually the best places to change money and cheques. Outside banking hours you'll have to use a bureau de change, which can be easily found at the airports and train stations and in larger cities. **Thomas Cook** and other major travel agents also operate bureaux de change with reasonable rates. Avoid changing money or cheques in hotels, as the rates are usually poor. Main post offices and branches of **Marks and Spencer** will change cash without charging commission.

Credit cards and ATMs

Most hotels, shops and restaurants accept the major credit cards though some places may charge for using them. Some smaller establishments such as B&Bs may only accept cash.

Currency cards

If you don't want to carry lots of cash, prepaid currency cards allow you to preload money from your bank account, fixed at the day's exchange rate. They look like a credit or debit card and are issued by specialist money changing companies, such as **Travelex** and **Caxton FX**. You can top up and check your balance by phone, online and sometimes by text.

Money transfers

If you need money urgently, the quickest way to have it sent to you is to have it wired to the nearest bank via **Western Union**, T0800-833833, www.westernunion.co.uk, or **MoneyGram**, www.moneygram.com. The Post Office can also arrange a MoneyGram transfer. Charges are on a sliding scale; so it will cost proportionately less to wire out more money. Money can also be wired by **Thomas Cook**, www.thomasexchangeglobal.co.uk, or transferred via a bank draft, but this can take up to a week.

Taxes

Most goods are subject to a Value Added Tax (VAT) of 20%, with the major exception of food and books. VAT is usually already included in the advertised price of goods. Visitors from non-EU countries can save money through shopping at places that offer Tax Free Shopping (also known as the Retail Export Scheme), which allows a refund of VAT on goods that will be taken out of the country. Note that not all shops participate in the scheme and that VAT cannot be reclaimed on hotel bills or other services.

Cost of travelling

England can be an expensive place to visit, and London and the south in particular can eat heavily into your budget. There is budget accommodation available, however, and backpackers will be able to keep their costs down. Fuel is a major expense and won't just cost an arm and a leg but also the limbs of all remaining family members, and public transport – particularly rail travel if not booked in advance – can also be pricey, especially for families. Accommodation and restaurant prices also tend to be higher in more popular destinations and during the busy summer months.

The minimum daily budget required, if you're staying in hostels or camping, cycling or hitching (not recommended), and cooking your own meals, will be around £30 per person per day. If you start using public transport and eating out occasionally that will rise to around £35-40. Those staying in slightly more upmarket B&Bs or guesthouses, eating out every evening at pubs or modest restaurants and visiting tourist attractions can expect to pay around £60 per day. If you also want to hire a car and eat well, then costs will rise considerably to at least £75-80 per person per day. Single travellers will have to pay more than half the cost of a double room, and should budget on spending around 60-70% of what a couple would spend.

Opening hours

Businesses are usually open Mon-Sat 0900-1700. In towns and cities, as well as villages in holiday areas, many shops open on a Sun but they will open later and close earlier. For banks, see above. For TIC opening hours, see the tourist information sections in the relevant cities, towns and villages in the text.

Post

Most post offices are open Mon-Fri 0900 to 1730 and Sat 0900-1230 or 1300. Smaller sub-post offices are closed for an hour at lunch (1300-1400) and many of them operate out of a shop. Stamps can be bought at post offices, but also from many shops. A 1st-class letter weighing up to 100 g to anywhere in the UK costs 60p (a large letter over 240 mm by 165 mm is 90p) and should arrive the following day, while 2nd-class letters weighing up to 100 g cost 50p (69p) and take between 2-4 days. For more information about Royal Mail postal services, call T08457-740740, or visit www.royalmail.com.

Safety
Generally speaking, England is a safe place to visit. English cities have their fair share of crime, but much of it is drug-related and confined to the more deprived peripheral areas. Trust your instincts, and if in doubt, take a taxi.

Telephone → *Country code +44.*
Useful numbers: operator T100; international operator T155; directory enquiries T192; overseas directory enquiries T153. Most public payphones are operated by British Telecom (**BT**) and can be found in towns and cities, though less so in rural areas. Numbers of public phone booths have declined in recent years due to the ubiquity of the mobile phone, so don't rely on being able to find a payphone wherever you go. Calls from BT payphones cost a minimum of 60p, for which you get 30 mins for a local or national call. Calls to non-geographic numbers (eg 0845), mobile phones and others may cost more. Payphones take either coins (10p, 20p, 50p and £1), 50c, 1 or 2 euro coins, credit cards or BT Chargecards, which are available at newsagents and post offices displaying the BT logo. These cards come in denominations of £2, £3, £5 and £10. Some payphones also have facilities for internet, text messaging and emailing.

For most countries (including Europe, USA and Canada) calls are cheapest Mon-Fri between 1800 and 0800 and all day Sat-Sun. For Australia and New Zealand it's cheapest to call from 1430-1930 and from 2400-0700 every day. However, the cheapest ways to call abroad from England is not via a standard UK landline provider. Calls are free using **Skype** on the internet, or you can route calls from your phone through the internet with **JaJah** (www.jajah.com) or from a mobile using **Rebtel**. Many phone companies offer discounted call rates by calling their access number prior to dialling the number you want, including www.dialabroad.co.uk and www.simply-call.com.

Area codes are not needed if calling from within the same area. Any number prefixed by 0800 or 0500 is free to the caller; 08457 numbers are charged at local rates and 08705 numbers at the national rate.

Time
Greenwich Mean Time (GMT) is used from late Oct to late Mar, after which time the clocks go forward 1 hr to British Summer Time (BST).

Tipping
Tipping in England is at the customer's discretion. In a restaurant you should leave a tip of 10-15% if you are satisfied with the service. If the bill already includes a service charge, which is likely if you are in a large group, you needn't add a further tip. Tipping is not normal in pubs or bars. Taxi drivers may expect a tip for longer journeys, usually around 10%.

Tourist information
Tourist information centres (TICs) can be found in most towns. Their addresses, phone numbers and opening hours are listed in the relevant sections of this book. Opening hours vary depending on the time of year, and many of the smaller offices are closed or have limited opening hours during the winter months. All tourist offices provide information on accommodation, public transport, local attractions and restaurants, as well as selling books, local guides, maps and souvenirs. Many also have free street plans and leaflets describing local walks. They can also book accommodation for a small fee.

Museums, galleries and historic houses

Over 300 stately homes, gardens and countryside areas, are cared for by the **National Trust (NT)**, T0844-800 1895, www.nationaltrust.org.uk. If you're going to be visiting several sights during your stay, then it's worth taking annual membership, which costs £53, £25 if you're aged under 26 and £70 for a family, giving free access to all National Trust properties. A similar organization is **English Heritage (EH)**, T0870-333 1181, www.english-heritage.org.uk, which manages hundreds of ancient monuments and other sights around England, including Stonehenge, and focuses on restoration and preservation. Membership includes free admission to sites, and advance information on events, and costs £47 per adult to £82 per couple, under-19s free. **Natural England**, T0845-600 3078, www.naturalengland.org.uk, is concerned with restoring and conserving the English countryside, and can give information on walks and events in the countryside.

Many other historic buildings are owned by local authorities, and admission is cheap, or in many cases free. Most municipal art galleries and museums are free, as well as most state-owned museums, particularly those in London and other large cities. Most fee-paying attractions give a discount or concession for senior citizens, the unemployed, full-time students and children under 16 (those under 5 are admitted free in most places). Proof of age or status must be shown.

Finding out more

The best way of finding out more information is to contact VisitEngland (aka the English Tourist Board), www.visitengland.com. Alternatively, you can contact VisitBritain, the organization responsible for tourism. Both organizations can provide a wealth of free literature and information such as maps, city guides and accommodation brochures. Travellers with special needs should also contact VisitEngland or their nearest VisitBritain office. If you want more detailed information on a particular area, contact the specific tourist boards; see in the main text for details.

Visas and immigration

Visa regulations are subject to change, so it is essential to check with your local British embassy, high commission or consulate before leaving home. Citizens of all European countries – except Albania, Bosnia Herzegovina, Kosovo, Macedonia, Moldova, Turkey, Serbia and all former Soviet republics (other than the Baltic states) – require only a passport to enter Britain and can generally stay for up to 3 months. Citizens of Australia, Canada, New Zealand, South Africa or the USA can stay for up to 6 months, providing they have a return ticket and sufficient funds to cover their stay. Citizens of most other countries require a visa from the commission or consular office in the country of application.

The UK Border Agency, www.ukba. homeoffice.gov.uk, is responsible for UK immigration matters and its website is a good place to start for anyone hoping visit, work, study or emigrate to the UK. For visa extensions also contact the UK Border Agency via the website. Citizens of Australia, Canada, New Zealand, South Africa or the USA wishing to stay longer than 6 months will need an Entry Clearance Certificate from the British High Commission in their country. For more details, contact your nearest British embassy, consulate or high commission, or the Foreign and Commonwealth Office in London.

Weights and measures

Imperial and metric systems are both in use. Distances on roads are measured in miles and yards, drinks poured in pints and gills, but generally, the metric system is used elsewhere.

Contents

18 Dorset
    19   Shaftesbury and Sherborne
    21   Dorset Downs
    24   Bournemouth and Poole
    27   Isle of Purbeck
    29   Weymouth to Lyme Regis
    32   Listings

38 Salisbury and around
    39   Salisbury
    43   North of Salisbury
    44   South and west of Salisbury
    46   Listings

48 Winchester and around
    49   Winchester
    54   West of Winchester
    55   East of Winchester
    56   Listings

58 New Forest
    59   Arriving in the New Forest
    59   Places in the New Forest
    63   Listings

66 Isle of Wight
    67   Arriving on the Isle of Wight
    68   Northwest Wight
    70   Northeast Wight
    72   Southeast Wight
    74   South and west Wight
    76   Listings

Footprint features

41   Druids: Bronze Age to New Age
43   Cereal thrillers
60   Walks in the New Forest
71   The Shipping Forecast

Dorset, New Forest & Isle of Wight

Dorset

Dorset is little England at its most rural, cosy, and green. Apart from Bournemouth, which was always traditionally in Hampshire, it has no large conurbations. Its scenery embraces acres of rolling farmland, landscaped parks, and lots of small manor houses and castles, rather than a few big stately homes, all set beside villages with impossibly quaint names like Purse Caundle, Toller Porcorum or Hammoon, near Fiddleford. It also seems to have been a hotbed of Iron Age activity: every other hillock has been carved into a crumpled hill fort. And of course this is Thomas Hardy country. Its centre is Dorchester, the busy county town, where he became a fatalistic old curmudgeon and great poet, but the county is scattered with scenes memorably described in his novels. Hilltop Shaftesbury and warm-stoned Sherborne, with its astonishing abbey, are the two medieval market towns in the north. In the middle, the unpromisingly named 18th-century town of Blandford Forum proves to be anything but, a tasty backwater with a church and quirky costume collection. Bournemouth needs little introduction, a coastal boomtown on the site of the Victorians' favourite watering place, its hillside villas change hands for rocketing prices almost as quickly as polite Poole's next door. Across Poole Harbour, the Isle of Purbeck is the stonemason and quarryman's heartland, a strange and until relatively recently all but forgotten corner of the south coast. Now it's been designated a World Natural Heritage Site. No doubt the steam railway that goes puffing past one of the most popular ruined castles of them all at Corfe, and has long provided a regular service for locals across Purbeck to rum old Swanage on the coast, will soon be linked into the national rail network. On the freshly branded 'Jurassic Coast', the most popular spots are still the rock arches at Durdle Door and the beach at Lulworth Cove, but it's the wonder of Chesil Beach and the resort of Lyme Regis and its surrounding cliffs that have really earned the attentions of UNESCO.

Shaftesbury and Sherborne → *For listings, see pages 32-37.*

The old town of Shaftesbury overlooks the rich clay farmland of the Blackmore Vale from a sandstone spur jutting out of the rolling wooded hills and fields of Cranborne Chase. The scenery of these two prosperous areas competes for prizes in the best-tended category in the south of England. Cranborne Chase hides the exotic delights of the Larmer Tree gardens and the romantic ruins of Old Wardour Castle, as well as the little baroque delight of Chettle House. Shaftesbury lacks the confidence of mellow-stoned Sherborne on the other side of the Blackmore Vale, probably because Sherborne can still boast a spectacular old abbey. In between the two, the countryside is peppered with quaint manor houses, like those at Fiddleford and Purse Caundle, both open to the public.

Arriving in Shaftesbury and Sherborne

Getting there Shaftesbury is about two hours from London down the M3 and A303. Sherborne is 30 minutes further down the road. **National Express** ① *T08717-818178, www.nationalexpress.co.uk*, serves Shaftesbury and Sherborne by coach direct from London Victoria (3½ hours to four hours) but there is usually only one service a day. About one slow train an hour leaves London Waterloo for Gillingham (near Shaftesbury) and Sherborne, taking around 2½ hours. For details contact **National Rail Enquiries** ① *T08457-484950, www.nationalrail.co.uk*, or **Traveline** ① *T0871-200 2233, www.traveline.info*.

Getting around A fairly good network of local buses is run by the **Wiltshire and Dorset Bus Company** ① *T01202-673555, www.wdbus.co.uk*, but a car or bicycle are easily the most convenient ways of exploring the Blackmore Vale.

Tourist information Shaftesbury TIC ① *8 Bell St, T01747-853514, www.shaftesbury dorset.com, Apr-Oct daily 1000-1700; Nov-Mar Mon-Sat 1000-1700; Jan-Mar Mon-Wed 1000-1300, Thu-Sat 1000-1700*, will book accommodation for a £3 fee. **Sherborne TIC** ① *Digby Rd, T01935-815341, www.sherbornetown.co.uk, www.westdorset.com, Apr-Oct Mon-Sat 0900-1700, Nov-Mar Mon-Sat 1000-1500*, offers a free accommodation booking service.

Shaftesbury

Shaftesbury is an old town, dramatically positioned on a sandstone bluff overlooking the vale of Blackmore, 18 miles west of Salisbury down the A30. Famous for the view down **Gold Hill**, a steep old cobbled street lined with partly thatched cottages, the place has been continuously occupied since AD 880, growing up around a wealthy nunnery and royal abbey at the top of the hill. It owes its olde-worlde charm today to the more-or-less consistent use of local building materials ever since. In 1820 it was a pocket borough controlled by the Grosvenor family. They sold up in 1919, by which time Shaftesbury had become famous as a manufacturing centre for underwear buttons, but like most of the rest of Dorset, industry never really took hold here. It remains a quiet, old-fashioned market town, a little depressed since losing much of its passing trade along the A30 with the opening of the A303 bypass in the 1960s. Gold Hill (its name a corruption of Guild Hall Hill), off the high street behind the Church of St Peter's, runs steeply down alongside the impressive remains of **Shaftesbury Abbey's precinct walls**, just along the ridge. A peak inside one of the quaint little houses on Gold Hill can be had at the volunteer-run

Shaftesbury Gold Hill Museum ① *Sun and Moon Cottage, Gold Hill, T01747-852157, www.goldhillmuseum.org.uk, Apr-Oct daily 1030-1630*, which displays the byzant, central to the history of the town's water supply, and some locally made firedogs, ladles and a trivet. The walk along the top of the hill is certainly memorable, to the site of the **Old Abbey** ① *T01747-852910, www.shaftesburyabbey.org.uk, museum and garden Apr-Oct 1000-1700, £3, concessions £2.50, under-16s free*. Although not much remains of it now, the museum here does a very good job of explaining its former importance – founded by Alfred the Great, it became the wealthiest Benedictine nunnery in the land – and the lives of the community that lived here.

Around Shaftesbury

Northeast of Shaftesbury, a couple of miles southwest of Tisbury, stands the empty shell of Lord Lovel's six-sided 14th-century castle, next to a lake in beautiful gardens. Designed to impress, the **Old Wardour Castle** ① *(EH), T01747-870487, www.english-heritage.org.uk, Apr-Sep daily 1000-1800, Oct daily 1000-1700, Nov-Mar Sat-Sun 1000-1600, £4.10, concessions £3.70, child (5-15) £2.50*, was damaged in the Civil War, and now contains a display on the life of the castle in its heyday.

South of Old Wardour, over Winklebury Hill fort and near the superb views from the top of the downland ridge at Win Green in the middle, stretch the green acres of the old royal hunting grounds of **Cranborne Chase**. At the mystical-sounding **Larmer Tree Gardens** ① *T01725-516225, www.larmertreegardens.co.uk, Mar-Oct Sun-Thu 1100-1630 (usually closed in July and early Aug for ticket-only music festivals), £4, concessions £3, child (5-14) £2.50*, the exotic park created by General Pitt Rivers in 1880 has been carefully restored along with its eccentric collection of garden buildings. These include a roman temple, an open-air theatre and various oriental and colonial pavilions. It's quite magical. Nearby is another rare thing, a small English baroque country house, **Chettle House** ① *Chettle, near Blandford Forum, T01258-830858, www.chettlehouse.co.uk, 5 and 12 May, 2 and 9 Jun, 4 and 11 Aug, 8 Sep, 1100-1700, £5, under 16s free*. Designed by Queen Anne's architect, Thomas Archer, with rounded corners and beautiful gardens, it has survived almost unmodified.

Sturminster Newton, 8 miles southwest of Shaftesbury, is a typical Dorset town, known locally as 'Stur'. Hardy called it Stourcastle, and moved here with his newly wed Emma in 1876 for a couple of the happiest years of their lives. Sturminster is connected to Newton by a six-arched medieval bridge over the River Stour. A mile to the east, a small part of a medieval manor house, with extraordinary roof structures and upper living room, has been preserved at **Fiddleford Manor** ① *(EH), Sturminster Newton, T0117-975 0700, www.english-heritage.org.uk, Apr-Sep daily 1000-1600, free*.

Sherborne

The jewel in Dorset's crown, Sherborne is set in a thickly wooded valley amid beautiful countryside immortally associated with the name of Digby. With its raised pavements and warm red Ham-stone houses, it has a very well-to-do air, despite being mistaken for Yeovil by German bombers in the Second World War. Digby Hill and Cheap Street are the two main shopping streets, but the pièce de résistance is its rusty-red old stone abbey. **Sherborne Abbey** was a cathedral until 1075 and displays a continuous procession of confident church-building up to the 15th century and the Reformation. Its Perpendicular fan vaulting is the astonishing highlight of the interior, as well as a variety of monuments (such as a full-length statue of the late 17th-century local squire John Digby) and the air of ancient peace. Sherborne town surrounds but does not hustle its abbey, fended off by some impeccably polite medieval almshouses. An interesting **antiques and fleamarket** ① *T01963-250108*, takes place on the fourth Saturday of each month in the Digby Church Hall up Digby Road opposite the abbey. Built by Sir Walter Raleigh in 1594, **Sherborne Castle** ① *T01935-813182, Easter-Sep Thu, Sat, Sun, bank holidays 1230-1700,* is the Digby family seat but it's not really a castle at all, more of a big old house beside a lake. The real thing is half a mile east of town: the 12th-century ruins of **Sherborne Old Castle** ① *(EH), T01935-812730, www.english-heritage.org.uk, Apr-Jun daily 1000-1700; Jul-Aug daily 1000-1800; Sep-Nov daily 1000-1700, £3.60, concessions £3.20, child (5-15) £2.20,* also inhabited by Raleigh, once took Cromwell over a fortnight to capture during the Civil War.

Dorset Downs → *For listings, see pages 32-37.*

The centre of Dorset is Hardy country through and through. Dorchester, the county town, in the south, is separated from the dignified backwater of Blandford Forum and the mini-cathedral town of Wimborne Minster by the last few vestiges of the novelist's beloved heaths. This is a landscape dominated by Iron Age hill forts. Maiden Castle, just outside Dorchester, is the largest in Europe. Others, like the Badbury Rings, Hambledon Hill and Knowlton, each have their distinctive qualities. Dorchester itself is a prosperous but not entirely prepossessing market town, milking the tourist dollar for all it's worth. Nearby, the carved hill figure wielding a club above his proud phallus draws the crowds to the little village of Cerne Abbas, while Milton Abbas is a very dinky set of thatched 18th-century cottages next door to another amazing abbey.

Arriving at the Dorset Downs
Getting there Hardy country is most easily reached using the M3 and A31 via Ringwood. Wimborne Minster is about 1½ hours from London. From Wimborne, Blandford is another 20 minutes up the A350 and Dorchester another half an hour or so along the A31 and A35. Dorchester Wimborne and Blandford Forum can be reached by **National Express** ① *T08717-818178, www.nationalexpress.co.uk*, coach in one hour from Bournemouth. Dorchester South is on the **Southwest Trains** mainline to Weymouth from London Waterloo (2½ hours) but not many trains stop there. **Wessex Trains** from Bath and Bristol (two hours) to Weymouth call at Dorchester West. **Traveline** ① *T0871-200 2233, www.traveline.info.*

Tourist information Blandford Forum TIC ① *1 Greyhound Yard, T01258-454770, www.visit-dorset.com, open year-round Mon-Sat 1000-1500.*

Blandford Forum
The dignified town of Blandford Forum sits to the south of Cranborne Chase. To the southwest stretch the remains of the Dorset Downs, embracing Thomas Hardy's celebrated Egdon heath on the edge of the Isle of Purbeck. Blandford is a later Georgian version of Marlborough, very much of a piece in its 18th-century architecture, epitomized by the superb baroque **Church of St Peter and St Paul**. Like the town hall, it was designed by the local Bastard brothers, John and William, after the fire that razed Blandford in 1731.

The story of the great fire is told at **Blandford Town Museum** ⓘ *Bere's Yard, Market Place, T01258-450388, www.blandfordtownmuseum.org, Apr-Oct, Mon-Sat 1030-1630, free,* an endearing small town museum with displays on local agriculture and wildlife as well. Another, more eccentric museum can be found up the road from the church. The **Blandford Fashion Museum** ⓘ *Lime Tree House, The Plock, T01258-453006, www.the blandfordfashionmuseum.com, mid-Feb to Nov Thu-Sat, Mon 1030-1700, £4, £3.50 concessions, child (7-15) £1.50,* began as a remarkable collection of old-fashioned costumes collected by local woman the late Mrs Betty Penny. Today this beautiful Georgian mansion houses costumes from 1735-1980 including designer by Bruce Oldfield and a special exhibition about 'passion for patterns'. A tearoom is attached.

Techies may well be more interested by the **Royal Signals Museum** ⓘ *Blandford Camp, T01258-482248, www.royalsignalsmuseum.co.uk, Jan Mon-Fri 1000-1600, Feb-Oct Mon-Fri 1000-1700, Sat-Sun 1000-1600, £7.50, concessions £6.50, child (5-16) £5.50, family £22,* an enlightening exercise in Army PR, billing itself as a 'museum of interactive science and technology communications'. The displays and exhibitions include the Enigma codebreaking machine, how a radio works and the invention of Morse code.

Three miles northwest of Blandford Camp, **Hambledon Hill** boasts two Iron Age hill forts, superb views and a wonderful tract of wild oak woodland.

Wimborne Minster and around

Wimborne Minster lies 9 miles southeast of Blandford on the outskirts of Bournemouth. A venerable old town, the eponymous church is still the main draw: a miniature cathedral in a strange mixture of styles from Norman to Perpendicular on the outside, full of extraordinary tombs, effigies and wondrous peace on the inside. The town itself struggles to keep out of Bournemouth's way, but nostalgic adults and kids will enjoy the **Wimborne Model Town** ⓘ *King St, T01202-881924, www.wimborne-modeltown.com, Apr-Oct daily 1000-1700, £5.50, concessions £5, child (3-15) £4.50,* a replica one-tenth scale version of the town as it sort-of looked in the 1950s.

The most attractive route to Wimborne from Blandford, the B3082, passes beneath the **Badbury Rings**, yet another Iron Age hill fort. The Rings lie within the **Kingston Lacy Estate** ⓘ *(NT), T01202-883402, www.nationaltrust.org.uk, Mar-Oct Wed-Sun, bank holidays 1100-1700, £11.70, under-16s £5.85, family £29.25, gardens only £7, under 16s £3.50, no dogs allowed,* once the seat of the Bankes family (after they'd moved from the ruin of Corfe Castle). The grand 17th-century house was modified by the Victorian architect Sir Charles Barry and contains William Bankes' splendid art collection. Point-to-point horse races are held here in late February, March and early April.

Seven miles north of Wimborne, at **Knowlton**, a ruined Norman church stands in the middle of neolithic earthworks, an evocative symbol of paganism meeting Christianity. Three miles to the southeast, wide sweeping views of the sea can be seen from the church at **Chalbury**, with its quaint 18th-century interior, even though it's at least 10 miles inland. Three miles further up the rolling B3078 from Knowlton, the beautiful Elizabethan **Cranborne Manor** ⓘ *Cranborne, T01725-517248, www.cranborne.co.uk, Mar-Sep Wed 0900-1700, £6, concessions £5, child £1 (free for RHS members),* is a private manor house surrounded by exceptionally pretty gardens: a series of 'outdoor rooms' divided by old yew hedges, originally laid out by John Tradescant and significantly enlarged in the 20th century.

West of Blandford Forum

On the edge of Hardy's heath, almost halfway from Blandford on the road to the headquarters of Hardy Country at Dorchester, the now much prettified **Milton Abbas** is a ridiculously cute thatched estate village created from scratch in the 18th century, when the Earl of Dorchester decided to improve the view from his house. **Milton Abbey** is now a private school for boys. The medieval abbey church was transformed to spectacular effect by Augustus Pugin's glass for the south window in the 19th century. Worth a look for that alone, it's also set in sweeping parkland next to the grand house that the architect William Chambers described as "terribly ugly".

Dorchester and around

Hardy's 'Casterbridge' and Dorset's county town is an old market town with attitude, wooing tourists with a shameless variety of attractions, the strangest of all being run by **World Heritage Ltd,** some more successfully than others. On the outskirts of town, is the site of Prince Charles's surreal experiment in town-planning at **Poundsbury.** The prince no doubt regrets that the town's single main street will be almost unrecognizable to readers of *The Mayor of Casterbridge* but Hardy fans can find plenty of solace elsewhere: **Max Gate** ⓘ *(NT), Alington Av, T01305-262538, Apr-Sep Mon, Wed, Sun 1400-1700 £2.40, under-16s £1.30,* was the house that he designed himself and lived in from 1885 until his death in 1928. The dining and drawing rooms can be seen, with some of his furniture. Better still, the **Dorset County Museum** ⓘ *High West St, T01305-262735, www.dorset countymuseum.org, Apr-Oct daily 1000-1700, Nov-Mar Mon-Sat 1000-1600, £6.50, up to 2 children free (under 15), additional child £3,* recreates his study, and tells the story of Maiden Castle and the local geology, flora and fauna in its wonderful old Victorian exhibition hall. The setting for Victorian and Georgian justice can be seen nearby at the **Old Crown Court and Cells** ⓘ *58-60 High West St, T01305-267992, www.westdorset.com; court room open with free entry for Tolpuddle Rally Festival on Sat 20 July 2013, 1000-1300, then Mon and Thu 22 Jul-29 Aug, 1400-1600; £2, children free,* where the Tolpuddle Martyrs (see page 29) were tried and transported.

Over the road, Dorchester's other attractions are harder to explain. The most recent addition is the **Terracotta Warriors Museum** ⓘ *High East St, T01305-266040, www.terracottawarriors.co.uk, daily 1000-1730, £5.99, under-16s £3.99,* which includes eight full-size Chinese-made replicas of the figures unearthed in 1976 in Xian. There's also a recreation of Tutankhamun's tomb and treasures in the **Tutankhamun Exhibition** ⓘ *High West St, T01305-269571, www.tutankhamun-exhibition.co.uk, daily Apr-Sep 1000-1700, Oct-Mar 1000-1600, £8.99, under-16s £6.99,* the most popular attraction in town; a **Dinosaur Museum** ⓘ *Icen Way, T01305-269741, www.thedinosaurmuseum.com, daily Apr-Sep 1000-1700, Oct-Mar 1000-1600, £6.99, under-16s £5.50*; and a **Teddy Bear Museum** ⓘ *Eastgate, corner of High East St and Salisbury St, T01305 266040, www.teddy bearmuseum.co.uk, daily Apr-Sep 1000-1700, Oct-Mar 1000-1600, £5.99, under-16s £3.99.* Further information can be found at www.world-heritage.co.uk.

Views over the town can be had from the extensive **Military Museum** ⓘ *T01305-264066, www.keepmilitarymuseum.org, Apr-Sep Mon-Sat 1000-1700; Oct-Mar Tue-Fri 1000-1630, £6.50, child £2.50, under-8s free.* The mighty mock-medieval Victorian castle gate now houses medals, machine guns and interactive displays.

Escaping from Dorchester itself, a variety of less carefully stage-managed attractions may prove more rewarding. A mile to the south, **Maiden Castle** is the mother of all hill forts, the largest in Europe and astonishing proof of our early ancestors' ability to shape the landscape to their own ends. Apparently it would have been home to about 200 families, quite possibly fiercely resistant to the Roman invasion of AD 43 but incapable in their isolation of joining up with other tribes to be effective in the struggle. The evidence of their colonization is the site of a Roman temple within the earth ramparts.

Seven miles north of Dorchester on the road to Sherborne, the delightful little village of **Cerne Abbas** is regularly overwhelmed in summer with visitors to the site of the country's most famous hill figure: the priapic Cerne Abbas giant. Sadly this extraordinary chalk figure, fully aroused and wielding his club, is more likely to be Roman than Celtic. It's now in the careful hands of the National Trust, which discourages couples from copulating on the chalky phallus by moonlight in the time-honoured tradition. The National Trust also looks after Thomas **Hardy's birthplace** ① *3 miles northeast of Dorchester, T01305-262366 mid-Mar to Oct Mon-Thu, Sun 1100-1700, £2.80,* a small cottage in Higher Bockhampton, little altered since being built by his great grandfather. Four miles east, on the edge of the Isle of Purbeck – and the remains of Hardy's wild Egdon Heath at **Affpuddle** – the Elizabethan manor house at **Athelhampton** ① *T01305-848363, www.athelhampton.co.uk, Mar-Oct Sun-Thu 1030-1700, Nov-Feb Sun 1030-dusk,* is still a family home with spectacular Victorian gardens.

Bournemouth and Poole → *For listings, see pages 32-37.*

Bournemouth, the grand dame of the South Coast, is enjoying a second honeymoon. Miles of long golden sands and safe waters continue to lure holidaymakers from far and wide to its sturdy cliffside seaside attractions as they have done since it first drew the steam-railway crowds in 1870. Recently recast as a more upmarket sunshine resort, Bournemouth's clean-cut and rather staid image – compared to its bohemian rival Brighton – has suddenly caught on. Since horticultural fashions have become all the televised rage, Bournemouth's generous array of immaculate Victorian gardens makes it a year-round choice for big firms and pre-retirement types. It's a city with all the mod cons within commuting distance from London, proudly expanding its position between the south coast's ring roads and the ferry ports, making it the leafy and upwardly mobile place to be. Villa-lined valleys slope towards the sea boasting house prices that would make even Londoners think twice. Youth culture has also arrived with the new prosperity and the town looks set to give Brighton a run for its money.

Arriving in Bournemouth
Getting there Bournemouth is very well connected to London via the M3 then M27. The journey from London takes under two hours. **National Express** ① *T08717-818178, www.nationalexpress.com*, runs 16 coaches a day between Bournemouth, Poole and London, with connecting services to Wareham, Corfe Castle, Swanage, Wareham, Dorchester and Weymouth.

Bournemouth train station greets the passenger with its impressive original iron and glass arch. **First Great Western** ① *T08457-000125, www.firstgreatwestern.co.uk*, runs services between London and Weymouth, Dorchester, Blandford Forum and Wimborne. **South West Trains** ① *T0845-600 0650, www.southwesttrains.co.uk*, run on the mainline to

Weymouth from London Waterloo taking around two hours, also calling at Southampton. For details contact **National Rail Enquiries** ① *T08457-484950, www.nationalrail.co.uk,* or **Traveline** ① *T0871-200 2233, www.traveline.info.*

Getting around Bournemouth is a relatively small place, much of which can be explored on foot or by bus or bicycle, though the city's hills can make it tough on the legs. The **City Sightseeing** buses operate here for guided tours, www.city-sightseeing.com, or the whole seafront can be explored by train and **cliff lift** ① *T01202-451781, www.bournemouth.co.uk, daily Easter-Oct (weather permitting), £1.20, under-16s 80p, family £3.80.* The West Cliff Lift links the seafront with the Bournemouth International Centre, the city's premier entertainment venue. The East Cliff Lift links the beach with the Russell Coates Art Gallery and Museum. The Fisherman's Walk Cliff Lift links the beach with a cliff-top café and children's play area. Local bus routes are run by **Yellow Buses** ① *T01202-636110, www.bybus.co.uk,* and **Wilts & Dorset Buses** ① *T0845-072 7093, www.morebus.co.uk.*

Tourist information Bournemouth TIC ① *Westover Rd, T0845-051 1700, www.bourne mouth.co.uk, Jul and Aug Mon-Sat 0930-1700, Sep-Oct 1000-1640, Nov-Mar 1030-1600.* **Poole TIC** ① *Poole Welcome Centre, 4 High St, T0845-234 5560, www.pooletourism.com, Nov-Mar 1000-1700, Sat 1000-1600, Apr-Jun, Sep-Oct daily 1000-1700, Jul-Aug daily 1000-1800.*

Background
Bournemouth was named by a Dorset squire, Lewis Tregonwell, who founded a summer home on the site of what is now the **Royal Exeter Hotel** in 1811. In 1837 Sir George Tapps-Gervis, a local landowner, established a resort next to the Tregonwell Estate, and Westover Villas, Westover Gardens and the **Bath Hotel** were all built. A jetty was built in 1856 which became the iron pier in 1880, and in 1866 the Arcade was built on the site of a rustic bridge crossing the Bourne stream. With the arrival of the railway, Bournemouth didn't look back, becoming the most successful seaside resort of the Victorian era on the south coast. The legacy of their solid and comfortable housing stock, and the fact that unlike elsewhere on this coast, much of it survived Second World War bombing, has contributed to the city's renaissance.

Places in Bournemouth
The centre of Bournemouth is a curious mix of concrete and heavy-handed modern architecture, side by side with swathes of abundant lush greenery and tailored Victorian arcades. The beachfront starts at the grand old **pier**, which houses an active theatre and traditional seaside sideshows (a carousel, a gaming arcade and a palm reader among others). Its view is unfortunately blighted by a spanking new Waterside development boasting a vast 3-D IMAX cinema, but the fun and excitement of the seaside remains undiminished.

The walk from the sea is cut up by the toughest of one-way systems, but the hordes can clamber up through the pleasantly cooling **Lower Gardens** to a mosaic-paved 'Square' and central Camera Obscura café which kick off the pleasant central pedestrian precinct. In Lower Gardens, wraparound views are also available from the **Bournemouth Balloon** ① *T01202-314539, www.bournemouthballoon.com, Mar-Oct 1000-2300, Nov-Feb Mon-Fri 1100-1700, Sat and Sun 1030-1800, £12.50, concessions £9.50, child £7.50,* offering 'the thrill of ballooning for a fraction of the cost of a hot-air flight'. The tethered balloon lifts up to 28 passengers 500 ft above sea level, giving panoramic views across town from Poole to the Isle of Wight. The original Victoriana shopfronts curve upwards in a distinctive hillside sweep and fans off into little arcades, each creating pockets of teenage excitement and domestic bustle down below.

Back on the ground level, the bigger department stores offer vast car parks and indoor watering holes. The open-air restaurants and old stores are nearly all madeover trendy bars and chic chain stores. The **Russell-Cotes Art Gallery & Museum** ① *East Cliff, T01202-451800, www.russell-cotes.bournemouth.gov.uk, Tue-Sun 1000-1700, Oct-Mar free, Apr-Sep £5, £4 child/concession,* is an awarding-winning museum, restored with Heritage Lottery funding, displaying a wealth of famous Victoriana, as well as Japanese artefacts and contemporary art exhibitions.

The seafront itself teems with all the usual attractions. The **Oceanarium** ① *seafront, T01202-311993, www.oceanarium.co.uk, daily 1000-1800, £9.95, concessions £8.50, child 3-15 £6.50, family £25.50,* boasts more than 10,000 sea creatures and also a charming 'turtle beach café'. Watch sharks, turtles and rays being fed daily. **Bournemouth Pier** ① *T01202-451781,* is an old-fashioned iron pier, with a theatre and mini-funfare at the end. It's the place to book local boat trips such as the Grand Firework Cruise, Scenic Tour to Sand Banks, Poole Harbour or 'Old Harry' Rocks and Swanage. Prices and times vary. A real draw is **Shockwave** ① *T0845-4684640, www.dorsetcruisecompany.co.uk, £8.50,* an 880 HP jet boat that bounces up to 12 passengers across the waves.

The best beaches, although always crowded in summer, are **Sandbanks**, **Branksome Chine**, **Flaghead** and **Alum Chine**. Bournemouth was home to the very first beach hut in 1909 which is still for rent today just east of the pier by the Bournemouth Beach Office. Alternatively you can hire a smart new beach hut beside the award-winning playground at **Alum Chine** with its deluxe paddling pool. Of the 1800 beach huts from Alum Chine to Southbourne, some 250 are hired out to the public costing from around £8 per day in low season (1 October-26 March) to £29 a day in summer. Contact the **Bournemouth Seafront Office** ① *Undercliff Drive, T01202-451781,* or visit www.bournemouthbeachhuts.co.uk.

Alternatively visitors can head east to Boscombe's trendy **Overstrand**, www.bournemouth.co.uk, overlooking the new artificial surf reef, which now has designer beach pods. Designed by Wayne and Gerardine Hemingway MBE of Red or Dead fame, there are 17 single pods for rent, each a work of art in its own right. Each has a wall of vintage coastal artwork inspired by the 1950s architecture of the Overstrand.

Poole

A polite harbour extension of Bournemouth, Poole lives up to its name thanks to Sandbanks and the Isle of Purbeck creating tranquil Poole Harbour, with lovely **Brownsea Island** ① *(NT), T01202-707744, www.nationaltrust.org.uk/brownsea-island,* in the middle, one of the last refuges of the red squirrel. In the town itself, **Poole Museum** ① *4 High St, T01202-262600, www.boroughofpoole.com/museums, Apr-Oct Mon-Sat 1000-1700, Sun 1200-1700; Nov-Mar Tue-Sat 1000-1600, Sun 1200-1600, free,* has a snazzy modern entrance leading to four floors of galleries housed in a 19th-century quayside warehouse. Displays cover everything from archaeology, art, pottery and pirates. Highlights include the Iron Age Poole logboat and the replica bird hide.

The **Study Gallery** ① *Poole College, North Rd, Parkstone, T01202-205200,* is home to Bournemouth and Poole College's important mid-20th-century art collection, with works by Henry Moore, Barbara Hepworth and Bridget Riley. Poole is also the official start of the **South West Coast Path** ① *T01752-896237, www.southwestcoastalpath.org.uk,* the longest and arguably most attractive National Trail in the UK.

Isle of Purbeck → *For listings, see pages 32-37.*

Not strictly an island, the Isle of Purbeck is a delightful stretch of chalky upland that drops into the sea in the east beside the funny old seaside town of Swanage. This is quarry country, the coast bearing witness to centuries of stone extraction and recently blessed with the grand designation of World Natural Heritage Site, the first of its kind in the country. Branded the Jurassic Coast, the ancient rock formations between Durlston Head and Weymouth have been pulling in the crowds for some time. The most popular sections are the limestone sea arch at Durdle Door and crescent bay of Lulworth Cove, although the whole coastline is well worth exploring. As well as being great walking country, the Isle of Purbeck also hides good wet-weather curiosities such as Lawrence of Arabia's retreat at Clouds Hill, stately Lulworth Castle's renovated shell and the Bovington Tank Museum.

Arriving in the Isle of Purbeck
Getting there The town is about 20 minutes's drive west of Poole on the A351. Swanage would take at least another 30 minutes to reach, possibly more in high season when Purbeck's roads can become congested. Wareham is on the main line to Weymouth from London via Bournemouth and Poole. A regular and very good-value steam train service runs from Norden, 3 miles south of Wareham, via Corfe Castle to Swanage.

Tourist information Swanage TIC ① *Shore Rd, T01929 423636, www.swanage.gov.uk. Apr-Sep Mon-Fri 1000-1300, 1400-1600.*

Wareham to Swanage
The main town at the entrance to the Isle of Purbeck, **Wareham**, is a solid, well-to-do market town with a prosperous air on the banks of the rivers Piddle and Frome. Boats can be hired from its old bridge, and beautiful walks across the floodplain of the Frome head towards its mouth in Poole Harbour. In the distance rise the Purbeck Hills, with the dramatic ruins of **Corfe Castle** ① *(NT), T01929-481294, www.nationaltrust.org.uk/corfe-castle, http://corfe-castle.co.uk, Apr-Oct daily 1000-1800, Nov-Feb daily 1000-1600, Mar daily 1000-1700, £7.72, under-16s £3.86, family £19.31,* sitting on a small mound in their central gap. A Norman and early English castle which once commanded the entire island, it was destroyed in the Civil War. Now one of the most popular and extraordinarily situated ruins in the country, it's often overrun with visitors in season playing hide and seek and scrambling up and down its grassy flanks.

Just north of Corfe Castle on the Wareham Road, Norden is the jumping-off point for the superb **Swanage Steam Railway** ① *T01929-425800, www.swanagerailway.co.uk, mid-Mar to Oct daily, Nov-Dec weekends, £6 return,* which runs via Corfe Castle, Harmonds Cross and Herston, to Swanage. There are wonderful views of Nine Barrows Down on the left. From Swanage, there's a great breezy ridge walk (4 miles) back to Corfe Castle across the neolithic burial mounds.

Swanage and Durlston Head

Swanage is one of England's most endearing seaside towns, just out of the way enough not to be completely ruined by the hordes. It does all the usual seaside things in a mini way, with regular visits from the steam paddleship *Waverley* in the summer. The town hall boasts a baroque façade originally from the Mercer's Hall in Cheapside, and various other bits of old London were collected and brought down here by the indefatigable George Burt in the 19th century. The most rewarding of his eccentric collection can be found after the stiff walk up out of town to the south, on Durlston Head, a great big globe of Portland Stone. **Durlston Head** is the most easterly point of the World Heritage Site now branded the Jurassic Coast as far as Exmouth. The first natural World Heritage Site in Britain, it celebrates the variety of rocks Triassic (200-250 million years old), Jurassic (140-200 million years old) and Cretaceous (65-140 million years old) and the unique forms, fossils, flora and fauna they have created and supported. The most spectacular of its geological features are the sea arches and rock stacks at Durdle Door and the extraordinary shingle bank of Chesil Beach (see page 30). Less obvious features include ripple marks on the rocks around Osmington that suggest Dorset once enjoyed a Bahaman climate and the fossil forest just east of Lulworth Cove.

St Aldhelm's Head to Lulworth Cove

From Durlston Head, a superb 5-mile stretch of the **South West Coast Path** runs along to **St Aldhelm's Head**. A couple of miles along, at **Dancing Ledge**, there's a swimming pool blasted out of the spectacular rocks by quarrymen. All along here, the quarries have left their mark, the stone being loaded at great risk into boats beside vertical walls of rock. Swimming in the sea along here is still only for the brave. **Seacombe** has a good rocky beach, and so does **Winspit**, just before steps lead up onto the wild and lonely **St Aldhelm's** or **St Alban's Head** itself. An atmospheric Norman chapel, a coastguard's lookout and cottages brave the southwesterlies in this desolate spot, although quiet valleys filled with gorse and blackberry bushes run inland to the little village of **Worth Matravers**.

Continuing along the coast path, beyond the eerie quiet of **Chapman's Pool**, a seaweed filled bay, you arrive after 4 miles in **Kimmeridge**, a popular spot with surfers. The Clavel Tower on the headland was built in 1820. The path on from here is at the discretion of the MOD, who use this beautiful 6-mile shoreline for target practice. The walks are usually open at weekends and during school holidays, but it's worth contacting the Lulworth Range Information Officer ① *T01929-404819*, to check. He should also be able to provide information as to the accessibility of **Tyneham**, the village requisitioned by the army at the start of the Second World War and never given back. Its story and that of the surrounding area has been vividly told by Patrick Wright in his book *The Village that Died for England*. As well as the tumbledown old cottages, schoolroom and manor houses, there are impressive walks out onto the headland and beach at **Worbarrow Tout** from here. Overlooking the ranges on the tiny road between East Creech and Lulworth, the **Franklin Viewpoint** commands a tremendous coastal panorama.

Lulworth Cove itself, 3 miles west of Tyneham, is a picturesque semicircle of sandy beach beneath the cliffs that can become impossibly crowded in summer. Almost as popular is **Durdle Door**, with its famous sea arch and beaches beneath Chaldon Down with views of Weymouth and the Isle of Portland. A little inland, **East Lulworth** village was moved in the 1780s by the Catholic Weld family, to clear the view from Lulworth Castle. Originally built as a very grand Jacobean hunting lodge, **Lulworth Castle** ① *T01929-400352, www.lulworth.com, Sun-Fri 1030-1600, £5, under-16s £3,* was converted spectacularly into a country house in the 18th century and equally spectacularly went up in flames in the 1920s. The shell has been restored by English Heritage at great expense. The **Great Chapel of St Mary's** close by was built in 1786, apparently the first free-standing Roman Catholic chapel to be built after the Reformation, allowed by George III "on the condition that it looked more like a mausoleum than a chapel". Various events, such as jousting and falconry, take place throughout the summer. The family-oriented **Camp Bestival** now takes place at Lulworth Castle in early August (see Festivals, page 36).

Inland from Lulworth Cove

Three miles further inland, the **Bovington Tank Museum** ① *T01929-405096, www.tank museum.org, daily 1000-1700 (last admission 1630), £12.50, £9 concessions, £7.50 child (5-16), family £33,* has some 150 armoured vehicles on show, all undercover. Bovington Camp's most famous soldier was TE Lawrence 'of Arabia', under the pseudonym TE Shaw. He lived nearby in a cottage at **Clouds Hill** ① *(NT), T01929-405616, www.national trust.org.uk/clouds-hill, Apr-Oct Thu-Sun, bank holidays 1200-1700 (or dusk if earlier), £5.50, child £2.50.* The man indirectly responsible for the British Mandate in Palestine, by organizing the Arab resistance to Turkish occupation, lived here in retreat from 1925 until his death in a motorbike accident in 1935, 600 yds down the road, at the age of 46. His simply furnished home has been kept much as it was, without electric light.

Three miles north at **Tolpuddle**, six farm labourers were arrested in February 1834 for establishing the first trade union. They were tried in Dorchester and transported to Australia. Thomas Standfield's cottage, where they took their illegal oath, still stands next to the Methodist chapel. The history can be explored at the **Tolpuddle Martyrs Museum** ① *T01305-848237, www.tolpuddlemartyrs.org.uk, Apr-Oct Tue-Sat 1000-1700, Sun 1100-1730, Nov-Mar Tue-Sat 1000-1600, Sun 1100-1600, free.*

Weymouth to Lyme Regis → *For listings, see pages 32-37.*

The Jurassic Coast continues west of Weymouth – a jolly seaside resort in summer, a little sad in winter – past Portland Bill and on to Chesil Beach, a remarkable shingle strand braving the breakers beneath superb downland scenery. It's well worth heading inland to enjoy the surrounding countryside: tucked away down tiny lanes are hidden gems like Mapperton Gardens, Eggardon hill fort and villages lost in time such as Compton Valence and Punchknowle.

Arriving in Weymouth and Lyme Regis

Getting there By road, Weymouth is about 30 minutes beyond Dorchester on the A354. A car or bike is really the best way to explore the coast. Weymouth is the terminus for trains via Bournemouth and Poole (50 minutes) from London Waterloo (two hours 40 minutes) and also has direct services to Bath (two hours), Bristol (two hours 20 minutes) and Wales.

Weymouth

Weymouth has an attractive old Georgian seafront which has been somewhat hijacked by its own success. The sandy beach gets very busy in summer with Punch and Judy performances, Maggie's Donkeys and amusements by the prom. The blue-and-white deck chairs give lovely views out over the Purbeck coast. Other than the sea, Weymouth's star attraction is the **Sea Life Adventure Park** ① *T0871-222 6938, www.visitsealife.com, daily 1000-1700, £22.50 (£14.50 online), under 3s free*, which is well worth a visit. The new **Weymouth Sea Life Tower**, www.weymouth-tower.com, is a 53-m-high revolving observation tower offering panoramic views of the coast and **Portland Bill**, which was used extensively during the 2012 Olympic Games for sailing. Another mock island, the **Isle of Portland**, is a strange outcrop of rock that has long provided the stone for many of Britain's grandest buildings, including St Paul's Cathedral. Some of its old quarries have been turned into visitor centres. The best is the **Lighthouse Visitor Centre** ① *T01255-45156, www.trinityhouse.co.uk, Apr-Sep Sun-Thu 1100-1700 (last tour 1630), £4, child £3, family £10*, on its most southerly point. It's worth the trek out here for the fine views of **Chesil Beach**, a 7-mile strip of pebbles sheltering a lagoon rich in wildlife called The Fleet. The beach is not safe for swimming but good for walks.

The best views of Chesil's complete extent can be had from the top of the **Hardy Monument** ① *Black Down, NT currently closed for restoration*. Not a memorial to the novelist, but to Nelson's flag-captain on *HMS Victory* at Trafalgar, Sir Thomas Masterman Hardy.

Around Weymouth

Abbotsbury ① *T01305-871387, www.abbotsbury-tourism.co.uk, 2 Jan-20 Dec daily 1000-1800 (1600 in winter), £15, child (5-15) £10 to all 3 sites*, is a thatched village near the coast that's almost too cute for its own good, with its swannery, subtropical gardens and

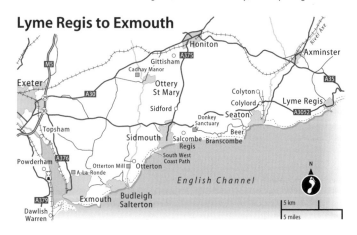

Lyme Regis to Exmouth

children's farm. A good view can be had by climbing up to **St Catherine's Chapel** perched on the top of the hill, with a turret once used as a lighthouse.

The coast road from Abbotsbury to **Bridport** is glorious, rolling through wild gorse and heather with the sea shining bright down below. The coastal settlements themselves are a little disappointing, although Bridport's seaside village at **West Bay** has a couple of good restaurants and a little harbour. It's best to press on to Lyme Regis or head inland to visit **Eggardon Hill**, a spectacular Iron Age hill fort, or **Mapperton Gardens** ① *T01308-862645, www.mapperton.com; gardens and All Saints Church, Mar-Oct daily except Sat, 1100-1700, £6, child (6-18) £3; house 8 Jul-9 Aug Mon-Fri, by pre-booked guided tour, £6, £3 child*, near Beaminster. The ornamental lakes and terraces are set in a spellbinding valley beneath a crumbling old manor house, with a little church and tearoom barn.

Lyme Regis

Lyme Regis may not quite live up to being twinned with St George's, Bermuda, but it's undeniably very pretty. Approached through rolling woodland on the coast road, this little fishing village was the setting for John Fowles' *French Lieutenant's Woman* and has a sandy dog-free beach at low tide. Its **Marine Parade** was the first public prom created in England, in 1771, the lower part being a cart road. The rebellious Duke of Monmouth landed here in 1685 and Jane Austen was fond of the place a century later. More interestingly, Mary Anning 'the Fossil Woman' discovered the Icthyosaurus in the fossil-encrusted cliffs here. The base is lower Jurassic topped by younger rocks and cliffs created by continual landslips. She invented the word 'dinosaur' and has even been immortalized in the tongue-twister 'she sells sea shells on the sea shore'.

The origins of Lyme Regis stretch back to the eighth century when monks distilled salt from the seawater here. Today, people enjoy strolling along the prom and up the town's impossibly quaint little streets and looking out over the **Cob**, the medieval harbour wall. If you're lucky, you might catch artist Adrian Gray (T01297-445062, www.stone balancing.com) in his signature India Jones hat, creating stone balancing sculptures on the pebbly beach. At its tip, the **Marine Aquarium** ① *T01297-444230, www.lymeregis marineaquarium.co.uk, Mar-early Nov daily 1000-1700, £5, child £4.50*, is a sweet little display of sealife, as well as wreckage, fishing gear and old photographs. A highlight is handfeeding the mullet. There are great views out to Portland along Chesil Beach and it's possible to take a trip out to see the Jurassic Coast by boat. Try **Lyme Regis Mackerel Fishing & Deep Sea Fishing Boat Trips** ① *T0797-479 6002, www.lymeregis.org/have_fun/boat_trips*. For anyone with kids, it's well worth checking with the TIC when the lifeboat station will be showing off its extraordinary sea-tractor.

Dorset listings

For hotel and restaurant price codes, and other relevant information, see pages 9-12.

⊖ Where to stay

Shaftesbury and Sherborne *p19*

££££ Stock Hill Country House,
Gillingham, near Shaftesbury, T01747-823626, www.stockhillhouse.co.uk. Gracious 1830s Victorian-built country house set in 11 acres of grounds, with landscaped gardens, tennis and croquet. Convenient for visiting local attractions.

£££ Plumber Manor, Sturminster Newton, T01258-472507, www.plumbermanor.co.uk. Homely family-run hotel with a good traditional restaurant in a delightful Jacobean manor house with garden crossed by the Devilish stream. Rooms are in the main house and in the converted stables.

££ Benett Arms, Semley, near Shaftesbury, T01747-830221, www.benettarms.co.uk. Friendly 3-storey pub on the green with with 5 en suite rooms. The restaurant does English favourites using local ingredients, such as Wiltshire ham and ploughman's lunches.

££ The Lamb, Hindon, T01747-820573, www.boisdale.co.uk/lamb-at-hindon. Rooms above a jolly country pub in the attractive village of Hindon, Frenchified by its boulevard of limes. Reasonable pub grub.

Dorset Downs *p21*

££££ Summer Lodge Country House Hotel, Evershot, near Dorchester, T01935-482000, www.summerlodgehotel.co.uk. A charming 1789-built hotel with indoor swimming pool and spa. Expertly prepared local seafood, beef, pheasant, rabbit and game are on the menu.

£££ Yalbury Cottage Hotel & Restaurant, Lower Bockhampton, near Dorchester, T01305-262382, www.yalburycottage.com. Two 350-year-old cottages with pine-furnished rooms overlooking fields or the garden.

The restaurant specializes in local produce and makes its own bread and ice cream.

Bournemouth *p24*

There are countless hotels, B&Bs and self-catering holiday lets in both Bournemouth and Poole, many some way from the centre out towards Boscombe.

££££ The Royal Bath Hotel Bournemouth, Bath Rd, T0871-221 0204, www.britanniahotels.com. A definite top-of-the-range choice in Bournemouth.

£££ Bournemouth – East Cliff Court, East Overcliff Drive, T01202-554545, www.menzieshotels.co.uk/hotels/south-coast/bournemouth-east-cliff-court. Set in an endless row of hotels overlooking the sea, this peppermint green one stands out with its newly refurbished cool summer stucco front, stylish rooms, 4-star rating, private pool and waft of cocktails from the terrace.

£££ Langtry Manor, Derby Rd, T01202-553887, www.langtrymanor.co.uk. This Edwardian manor house was built by the Prince of Wales (King Edward VII) as a hideaway for his paramour, Lillie Langtry. All rooms have individual themes and are spacious. A beautiful dining hall with stained-glass windows and a gallery.

£££ The Norfolk Royale Hotel, Richmond Hill, T01202-551521, www.peelhotels.co.uk. Recently refurbished with 95 spacious suites in the centre of town near the attractive gardens and beach.

Poole *p26*

£££ The Haven, Sandbanks, T0845-337 1550, www.havenhotel.co.uk/haven/contact-hotel-poole-dorset. Great family hotel and spa with prime location on the exclusive Sandbanks Peninsula.

£££ Hotel du Vin & Bistro, Thames St, T08447-489265, www.hotelduvin.com/locations.poole. Part of the successful **Hotel**

du Vin boutique chain, this stylish hotel has 38 beautiful bedrooms and suites and a reliably good bistro and wine cellar.

££ The Antelope Inn, Old High St, T01202-672029, www.oldenglishinns.co.uk/poole. This old coaching inn boasts a 23 rooms, a carvery, cask-conditioned bitters and a fireplace dating from 1465. It's a lively place, once serving as a molasses store, a 19th-century judges court and a base for commando operations in the Second World War.

££ The Sandbanks Hotel, Sandbanks, T0845 3371550, www.sandbankshotel.co.uk. A great family-friendly hotel with direct access to Sandbanks' Blue Flag beach.

Isle of Purbeck *p27*

££££ The Alexandra Hotel, Pound St, Lyme Regis, T01297-442010, www.hotel alexandra.co.uk. In a knockout location overlooking Lyme Bay, this hotel has a cool English aesthetic.

££££-£££ The Pig on the Beach, above Studland Beach, T0845-077 9494, www.the pighotel.com/on-the-beach. Opens late 2013 with dramatic views over Old Harry Rocks and will feature a kitchen garden of home-grown produce and super-stylish rooms.

£££ Priory Hotel, Church Green, Wareham, T01929-551666, www.theprioryhotel.co.uk. Set on the banks of the River Frome, this 16th-century priory is peaceful and quiet. The owners have converted the former boathouse into 2 luxury suites. Rooms in the priory look onto the Purbeck Hills. The restaurant has moorings for diners arriving by boat.

££ Bradle Farmhouse, Bradle, near Church Knowle, T01929-480712, www.bradlefarm house.co.uk. Some comfortable rooms with en suite bathrooms in a delightful location near Corfe Castle.

££ Scott Arms, Kingston, T01929-480270, www.thescottarms.com. This trendy pub with rooms has tremendous views over Corfe Castle from its garden, good locally sourced food and stylish bedrooms. Breakfast included.

Weymouth to Lyme Regis *p29*
£££ Bay View Hotel, Marine Parade, Lyme Regis, T01297-442059, www.lyme bayhotel.co.uk. Right on the seafront, with a hip 1950s feel to it, and a very fresh fish restaurant.

£££ The Bull Hotel, 34 East St, Bridport, T01308-422878, www.thebullhotel.co.uk. Striking, family-friendly boutique hotel right on the high street.

£££ Manor Hotel, West Bexington, near Bridport, T01308-897660, www.manor hoteldorset.com. With flagstone floors, intricately carved panelling, a low ceiling cellar bar, stone walls and oak, this 16th-century stone building is an olde worlde kind of place. Rooms with sea views.

£££ Moonfleet Manor, Fleet Rd, Weymouth, T01305-786948, www.moon fleetmanorhotel.co.uk. Majestic family-friendly 5-star hotel known for its appealing shabby chic, overlooking Chesil Beach.

£££ Thatch Lodge Hotel, The Street, Charmouth, near Lyme Regis, T01297-560407. Thatch Lodge was built in 1320 as a resting place for monks. The rooms are all unique and the cooking is based on fresh local produce. The cottage has 200-year-old vines and hand-picked grapes.

££ Crafty Camping, Higher Holditch Farm, Holditch, T01460-221102, www.mallinson.co.uk. Glamping with sheepskins, shepherds' huts, sauna yurts, flossing loos and hot showers.

££ Melcombe Villa Guesthouse, Weymouth, T01305-783026, www.melcom bevilla.co.uk. A good central option, close to the beach.

🍽 Restaurants

Shaftesbury and Sherborne *p19*
££ The Crown, Fontmell Magna, near Shaftesbury, T01747-811441, www.thefontmell.com. Good selection of well-crafted meat, fish and vegetarian dishes. Boutique-style rooms above.

££ John Peel, 52 High St, Shaftesbury, T01747-853178. A good-value restaurant, with vegetarian options and generous portions. BYOB.

££ Rose and Crown, Trent, near Sherborne, T01935-850776, www.roseandcrown trent.co.uk. A good local pub with a large garden, and slightly fancy menu, but open fires and flagstone floors beneath the thatch.

££ The Ship Inn, Bleke St, Shaftesbury, T01747-853219, www.shipinnfree house.co.uk. An 'olde-worlde pubbe' in scenic Shaftesbury, with a refurbished 17th-century interior and boules pitch outside.

££ White Horse, Hinton St Mary, Sturminster Newton, T01258-472723. Home- made traditional English food on the menu for lunch and supper and a flower-filled garden with a lovely aspect. Book ahead at weekends.

££ Ye Olde Two Brewers, 24 St James St, Shaftesbury, T01747-854211, www.2brewers.co.uk. Great views and a wide variety of locally produced food on offer in a roomy pub off Gold Hill.

Dorset Downs *p21*
£££-££ The Wild Garlic, Iwerne Minster, Blandford Forum, T01747-811269, www.the wildgarlic.co.uk. Run by Masterchef winner and forager, Mat Follas. High standard fare served in the restaurant or more informally in the bar/grill. Also has 5 bedrooms.

££ The Acorn Inn, Evershot, near Dorchester, T01935-83228, www.acorn-inn.co.uk. Comfortable village pub with good food and rooms if you fancy staying.

££ The Crown, Ibberton, near Blandford, T01258-817448. Nestling in the Blackmoor Vale below Bulbarrow Hill, an old little pub with a large fireplace.

££ Frampton Arms, Moreton, T01305-852253, www.framptonarms.co.uk. Conveniently close to the station, in the village where TE Lawrence is buried, with wide menu of home-made food.

££ Hambro Arms, Milton Abbas, T01258-880233, www.hambroarms.com. Pool table and big log fires in the middle of thatched model village, also doing fresh local produce.

Bournemouth *p24*
££ Alcatraz Brasserie, 127 Old Christchurch Rd, T01202-553650, www.alcatraz.co.uk. Modern Italian dining in a cool elegant dining room with open-air patio overlooking the start of the gardens.

££ Aruba Restaurant & Bar, Pier Approach, T01202-554211, www.aruba-bournemouth.co.uk. This restaurant is in a prime position on top of the amusements, with a wraparound terrace. Family-friendly by day and clubby by night. Reliably good food.

££ Coriander, 22 Richmond Hill, T01202-552202, www.coriander-restaurant.co.uk. A Mexican eatery with a friendly local buzz, that beats the constant diet of seaside fish bars or big pick-up joints.

££ The Print Room, Echo Building, Richmond Hill, T01202-789 6669, www.theprintroom-bournemouth.co.uk. Sister restaurant to **Aruba**, housed in the former *Echo* newspaper offices, offers smart dining with a trendy edge.

££ West Beach, Pier Approach, T01202-587785, www.west-beach.co.uk. A fish and seafood restaurant that's a real summer find. Right on the beach it overlooks the pier and nestles under the cliff. The main restaurant offers mussels and fresh catch of the day in some Côte d'Azur style. There's even a separate deck right out over the beach, shading the beau monde from the scalding sun under its blue uniform umbrellas. Either side of the long windows are little outlets for the bikini-clad masses to purchase their dishes at takeaway prices, and the burgers and ices prove the popular favourite.

££-£ Urban Reef, Boscombe Pier, T01202-443960, www.urbanreef.com.

Fabulous modern restaurant right on the prom in front of Boscombe's artificial reef, with downstairs café, bar and deli and upstair restaurant. Cool, buzzy surf vibe throughout.

£ Delice des Champs, 13 Gervis Pl, T01202-319094. Everything French.

£ Harry Ramsden's, Undercliffe Drive, East Beach, T01202-295818, www.harryramsdens.co.uk. Established in 1928, "The World's Most Famous Fish & Chips" is an institution. Serving large helpings of fresh fish to take out or sit upstairs and enjoy a more sheltered view over the bathing beaches.

Poole *p26*

££ Hardy's Restaurant, 14 High St, T01202-660864. A family-owned bistro offering baked snapper in a friendly more authentic atmosphere.

££ John B's, 20 High St, Old Town, T01202-672440. Does French double-fronted dining offering snails and all the usual gourmand treats in a formal manner.

£ Oriel Café & Restaurant, The Quay, T01202-679833, www.orielpoole.co.uk. Summery white and cream suitable for families and high tea.

£ Shell Bay, Poole. A great spot overlooking the sea with resplendent dining rooms and patios serving delicious local seafood.

Isle of Purbeck *p27*

££ Fox Inn, West St, Corfe Castle, T01929-480449. Has log fires, views of the castle and daily specials on the menu.

£ Square and Compasses, Worth Matravers, T01929-439229, www.squareandcompass pub.co.uk. An unreconstructed old boozer with beer-through-the-hatch, basic snacks and regular live music of sorts, pretty much the heart of the headland. The landlord will probably find room for your tent if you ask nicely.

Weymouth to Lyme Regis *p29*

£££ Riverside Restaurant, West Bay, T01308-422011, www.thefishrestaurant-westbay.co.uk. Laid-back freshly prepared seafood restaurant right on the water. Booking advisable.

££ The Bridport Arms Hotel, West Bay, T01308-422994, www.bridportarms.co.uk. A thatched hotel beside the beach, with daily fish specials.

££ Crab House Café, Wyke Regis, T01305-788867, www.crabhousecafe.co.uk. Right on the Fleet between Weymouth and Portland Bill, finger lickingly good seafood.

££ Hive Beach Café, Burton Bradstock, T01308-897070, www.hivebeachcafe.co.uk. Caught-on-the-day seafood, busy in summer but well worth the effort.

££ Hix Oyster & Fish House, Lyme Regis, T01297-446910, www.hixoysterandfish house.co.uk. Fabulous oysters and Spanish wine.

££ Spyway Inn, Askerswell, near Bridport T01308-485250, www.spyway-inn.co.uk. Close to the impressive hill fort at Eggardon, good home-cooked food and superb views from the garden.

££ Three Horseshoes, Powerstock, T01308-485328, www.threeshoesdorset.co.uk. Excellent local produce and seafood with spacious gardens and panelled dining room in a working village.

££ The Watch House Café, West Bay, Bridport, T01308-459330, www.watch housecafe.co.uk. Set right on the beach with stunning Jurassic Coast views, this is a must for fresh seafood and wood fired pizzas.

⑪ Pubs, bars and clubs

Bournemouth *p24*

Aruba Bar, Pier Approach, T01202-554211, www.aruba-bournemouth.co.uk (see Eating). Great location.

The Brasshouse, 8-9 Westover Rd, T01202-589681. A vast cavernous pub in the day, with request DJs and grooves every night.

Daisy O'Briens, 77 Old Christchurch Rd, T01202-290002. A long way from Tipperary, but this old one-off Irish pub in the heart of the high-street shopping district offers a break from the chainstore stranglehold.

Goat and Tricycle, 22-29 West Hill, T01202-314220, www.goatandtricycle.co.uk. An old-fashioned place with reasonable pub grub and billiards.

Clubs

Bournemouth's club scene is hotting up. **Wave FM** on 105.2 plugs the local scene and most bars offer DJs in the evening and cater to students during term time.

Heroes, 284 Old Christchurch Rd, T01202-294668, www.heroesbournemouth.com. Bournemouth's only karaoke bar.

Poole *p26*

King Charles Pub, Thame St, T01202-566405. A traditional old tavern with low ceilings and hearty hot pot suppers.

Oyster Quay, Port Saint James, The Quay, T01202-668669. There's high summer fun with weekend DJs at this waterfront bar and grill, sporting live tropical fish behind the bar and biweekly firework displays.

Poole Arms, The Quay, T01202-672309. A burnished green tiled-fronted pub offering a friendly pint on the old harbour.

🐵 Entertainment

Bournemouth *p24*

Theatres, live music and comedy
Bournemouth International Centre (**BIC**) and **Pavillion Theatre**, box office T0844-576 3000, www.bic.co.uk/events. Bournemouth's premier entertainment venues. The Pavilion is the original home of the Bournemouth Symphony Orchestra opened in 1929 and includes a 1600-seat theatre, ballroom, restaurant and terraces overlooking the Lower Gardens. This thriving theatre offers tours, ballroom dancing, afternoon tea dances, country line dancing, lunchtime organ concerts, balls, military tattoo, and touring concerts and events.

Forest Arts Centre, Old Milton Rd, New Milton, Hampshire, T01425-612393, www3.hants.gov.uk/forest. A few miles east of Bournemouth this thriving arts centre is an arty alternative.

The Pier Theatre, Pier Approach, T01202 306126. Literally at the end of Bournemouth pier, full of holiday fun, offering respectable touring classics from Ayckbourne to Coward with the extra twinkle of a familiar TV celebrity cast in a leading role.

Poole *p26*

Bournemouth Symphony Orchestra, 2 Seldown Lane, Poole, T01202-669925, www.bsolive.com. An established touring orchestra, offers classical firework summer proms at local houses.

✿ Festivals

Shaftesbury and Sherborne *p19*
May Sherborne Town and Abbey Festival. Regular concerts on Sat nights in the Abbey.
Aug-Sep Great Dorset Steam Fair, Tarrant Hinton, near Blandford at the end of Aug and early Sep, T01202-456456, www.gdsf.co.uk. All the tackle and steam at the fair on a 500-acre site, widely renowned as the leading event of its kind in the world. Attracting the steam buff from miles around.

Bournemouth and Poole *p24*
Jul Boscombe Carnival, held 22-28 Jul. The Red Arrows make an annual appearance.
Jul-Aug Bournemouth Carnival, runs from 29 Jul-4 Aug.

Isle of Purbeck *p27*
Aug Camp Bestival, T0844-888 4410, www.campbestival.net. 4-day music and family entertainment festival in early Aug in the grounds of Lulworth Castle. Tickets cost £190, £113 child (15-17), £98 (11-14), under 10s free.

O Shopping

Bournemouth and Poole *p24*
Beales, The Granville Chambers,
21 Richmond Hill, T01202 552022,
www.beales.co.uk. The local department
store. After all the usual chains from Marks
& Spencer to Debenhams, the local favourite
remains this old staple.
BIC Purbeck Hall and Lounge,
Bournemouth, www.bic.co.uk. Something is
usually staged for the bric-a-brac hunter as
well as exhibitions from antiques fairs in the
Pavilion Ballroom to the Ideal Home Exhibition.
Quiksilver, 79 Old Christchurch Rd, T01202-
295412. Cheerful and trendy beachwear and
accessories, part of the south coast 'Just Add
Water' chain for designer surf-n-sun wear.
Westover Gallery, 4 Westover Rd, T01202-
297682, www.westovergallery.co.uk. Present
local artists and glassware in one of the
prettiest Victorian covered arcades.

▲ What to do

Bournemouth and Poole *p24*
AFC Bournemouth, www.afcb.co.uk.
For information on all forthcoming football
matches from the local team.
Brownsea Island Ferries, T01929-462383,
www.brownseaislandferries.com. "For
the perfect day out on the famous
yellow boats of Poole".
Poole Harbour Boardsailing,
284 Sandbanks Rd, Lilliput, Poole,
T01202-700503, www.pooleharbour.co.uk.
Poole Sea Angling Centre, rear of 5
High St, Poole, T01202-676597,
www.pooleseaanglingcentre.co.uk.

Self-Drive Boat Hire, Cobbs
Quay, Poole, T01202-687778,
www.purplepelicanboathire.co.uk.

Weymouth to Lyme Regis *p29*
Nature watching
New Forest Badger Watch, T01306-
863054, www.beaminsterbadgers.co.uk.
Apr-Nov badger watching.

⊖ Transport

Bournemouth and Poole *p24*
Bicycle
Action Bike, Dolphin Centre, Poole,
T01202-680123, www.action-bikes.co.uk;
On Yer Bike, 90 Charminster Rd,
Bournemouth, T01202-315855,
www.onyerbike.co.uk.

Car
Avis, 33-39 Southcote Rd, Bournemouth,
T01202-296942; **Europcar**, Upper Station
Approach, Bournemouth, T01202-293357.

Taxi
There is a taxi rank at Central Station,
Bournemouth, T01202-556166.

O Directory

Bournemouth and Poole *p24*
Hospital Bournemouth Nuffield Hospital,
67-71 Lansdowne Rd, Bournemouth,
T01202-291866.

Salisbury and around

Bordering Dorset to the east, the county of Wiltshire was apparently the homeland of the earliest human inhabitants of the British Isles and they made an impression on the landscape that has survived to this day. On Salisbury Plain, Stonehenge is the pièce de résistance of course with an impressive new visitors centre, although just one of a wealth of longbarrows, stone circles, tumuli and other earthworks dotted about the region. Seven miles to the south, the use of stone in the Middle Ages achieved one of its most dramatic expressions in the spire of Salisbury Cathedral, pointing skyward above a lively and beautiful market city surrounded by watermeadows and quiet little river valleys – surely one of England's most beautiful cities. To the South and West down in the Avon Valley, there are Elizabethan manor houses, countryside museums, Iron Age hill forts and cute thatched villages to explore.

Salisbury

Salisbury wins out in the league of beautiful cities of the south mainly because it has been lucky enough to keep out the way of big new road-building programmes – which comes as some surprise given that nine major old roads meet here near the confluence of four rivers on the banks of the River Avon. The Market Square is the centre of things, alive and busy every Tuesday and Saturday, while the Close and its cathedral remain very peaceful and serene behind their old walls a few hundred yards away. The cathedral, with its magnificent spire, is still the main event, although Salisbury is large enough to boast some thriving nightlife, characterful pubs and one of the best rep theatres in the south.

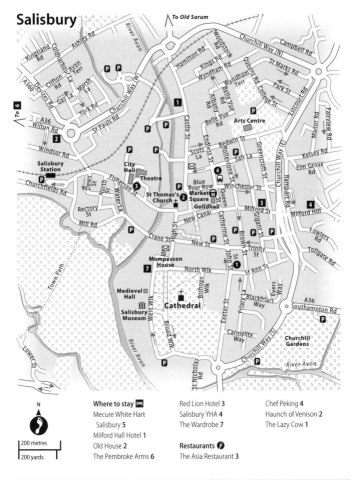

Where to stay 🛏
Mecure White Hart
Salisbury **5**
Milford Hall Hotel **1**
Old House **2**
The Pembroke Arms **6**

Red Lion Hotel **3**
Salisbury YHA **4**
The Wardrobe **7**

Restaurants 🍴
The Asia Restaurant **3**

Chef Peking **4**
Haunch of Venison **2**
The Lazy Cow **1**

Arriving in Salisbury

Getting there Relatively off the beaten track, Salisbury is about 7 miles south of the A303 between London and Exeter, and about 14 miles north of the A31 between London and Bournemouth. A major road junction itself, it's very easy to reach by car, taking on average 1½ from the M25. **National Express** ① *T08717-818178, www.nationalexpress.com*, runs three direct services from London Victoria daily (three hours). **South West Trains** ① *T0845-6000650, www.southwesttrains.co.uk*, runs an hourly service to Salisbury from London Waterloo, taking 1½ hours.

Getting around Salisbury city centre is small and charming enough to make walking around it a pleasure. Destinations out of town can be reached on **Wilts and Dorset Buses** ① *T01722-336855, www.wdbus.co.uk*.

Tourist information Salisbury TIC ① *Fish Row, T01722-342860, www.visitwiltshire.co.uk, Apr-Sep Mon-Fri 9000-1700, Sat 1000-1600, Sun 1200-1600; Oct-Mar Mon-Fri 0900-1700, Sat 1000-1500, Sun 1200-1500*, offers a free accommodation booking service.

Background

The Romans set up camp overlooking one of their most important crossroads on a small hill now known as Old Sarum. Sorbiodunum, as they called it, was conquered by the Saxons and called Searesburgh, which the Normans later called Searesbyrig, hence Salisbury. Old Sarum is still quite an extraordinary place to visit, partly because the settlement was abandoned completely in 1219 when the cathedral was relocated onto the plain below. Legend has it that Bishop Poore had an arrow fired from Old Sarum down into the valley and founded the new cathedral where it fell. Since then, Salisbury's history has been quiet and largely uneventful, something that its heritage industry today can be grateful for.

Places in Salisbury

Although most visitors are inevitably drawn towards the cathedral's towering spire, the city centre is also worth exploring. Unlike the twisting Saxon layout of Canterbury, the regular grid of old medieval streets around **Market Square** can reasonably claim to be one of the earliest examples of new town planning in Europe. Clearly Salisbury's Norman founders had learned a thing or two from the Romans. Dominated by the **Guildhall**, the square still lives up to its name on Tuesdays and Saturdays, at other times doing service as a fairly grand car park.

North of Market Square, Castle Street runs alongside the River Avon. To the east, Blue Boar Row leads into Winchester Street, one of the city's more intriguing shopping strips for antiques and other one-offs. Just to the west, **St Thomas's Church**, consecrated to Canterbury's Thomas à Becket, was founded in the 13th century, at the same time as the cathedral, but rebuilt in the 15th century. Inside, the chancel arch is decorated with a superb Doom painting, and there are medieval murals depicting the Annunciation, Visitation and Nativity as well as some fine pre-Reformation stained glass.

From St Thomas's Square, the High Street leads south to the **Close**, although St John Street provides the most satisfying approach to the cathedral. Pretty much undisturbed by the passing of time, the Close seems to be in a world of its own, its gates locked at

Druids: Bronze Age to New Age

When Julius Caesar invaded Britain in the first century BC he already knew from his experiences conquering Gaul that the Druids would give him trouble. Recent research suggests that these warrior priests presided over a settled and sophisticated agrarian Celtic community, probably undertaking most of the roles occupied by the professional classes today. They were doctors, lawyers and chartered surveyors all rolled into one. Indeed the Romans only finally crushed their resistance more than a century later at a bloody battle on Anglesey Island in Wales. Archaeologists have suggested that the siting of burial mounds and stone circles over former domiciles indicates that the Druids practised a religion that believed in an underworld peopled by their tribal ancestors. These monuments were taken to be the gateway to the land of the dead. Sadly the historical evidence is at odds

with the popular image of the priesthood epitomised by Getafix in the Asterix cartoons. Rather than wandering affably around in search of mistletoe with their golden sickles, they're more likely to have been found ritually garotting young men – the probable fate of Lindow Man, now preserved in the British Museum – and instilling their followers with a casual lack of concern for personal safety, something that bothered the Roman legionaries. Modern Druids espouse a more limited faith – in the sanctity of the seasons and respect for mother nature, in the animistic spirits of wood and stream and in flowing facial hair.

It is these gentle although not entirely unprofessional souls that have earned the right to celebrate their faith at Stonehenge on the summer solstice each year and thankfully not their reincarnated Bronze Age brethren.

night, protecting the seclusion of residents such as former Conservative prime minister Edward Heath. The High Street entrance leads into Choristers Green, where stands **Mompesson House** ① *(NT), The Close, T01722-420980, Mar-Oct 1100-1700, £5.50, under-16s £2.75, garden only £1,* a stately Queen Anne building with a remarkable interior featuring some very fine plasterwork and oak staircase, as well as an 18th-century collection of drinking glasses, antique furniture and a walled garden. It featured as Mrs Jennings' home in Ang Lee's film adaptation of Jane Austen's *Sense and Sensibility*.

The **West Walk**, backing onto the watermeadows of Queen Elizabeth Gardens, is home to three engaging attractions that can satiate the most anoraky thirst for local history. The first is the most specialized and often the least overwhelmed: 'The **Wardrobe'** ① *58 The Close, T01722-419419, www.thewardrobe.org.uk, Feb Tue-Sat 1000-1700; Mar Mon-Sat 1000-1700; Apr-Sep Mon-Sat 1000-1700, Sun 1200-1630; Oct Mon-Sat, 1000-1700; Nov Tue-Sat 1000-1700, £4.50, concessions £3.50, under-16s £1.20,* is the Berkshire and Wiltshire Regiment's museum with beautiful gardens leading down to the river and water meadows. A few doors down, 'The Secrets of Salisbury' in the **Medieval Hall** ① *Sarum St Michael, West Walk, Cathedral Close, T01722-324731, www.medieval-hall.co.uk, open all year for pre-booked groups,* the old 13th-century dining hall of the Deanery – one of the oldest domestic buildings in the close – offers a 40-minute presentation. Next door, the **Salisbury Museum** ① *The King's House, 65 The Close, T01722-332151, www.salisburymuseum.org.uk, Mon-Sat 1000-1700 (also Jun-Sep*

Sun 1200-1700), £6, under-16s £2, is an excellent example of its type, complete with Stonehenge and Early Man Gallery, the Pitt Rivers Gallery – full of intriguing anthropological finds – the Brixie Jarvis Wedgwood Collection of almost 600 pieces of fine china, and an award-winning costume gallery called 'Stitches in Time'.

Opposite these three stands the perfection of the west front of the **cathedral** ① *visitor services: 33 The Close, T01722-555120; cathedral services information: T01722-555113, www.salisburycathedral.org.uk, daily 0715-1815 (because of services, recommended visiting times are Mon-Sat 0900-1700 and Sun 1200-1600), suggested donation £6.50, concessions £5.50, child (5-17) £3, family £15*. Along with St Paul's Cathedral in London and Truro in Cornwall, Salisbury is remarkable in representing the church-building achievement of a single generation. Sitting in probably the most beautiful and certainly the largest cathedral close in the country, it was built at miraculous speed between 1220 and 1258, in the style now known as Early English Gothic. Half a century or so later this great medieval palace of worship was blessed with a soaring 400-ft spire that has beautified distant views of Salisbury ever since. Famously portrayed by the painter John Constable as the centrepiece of a quintessentially English landscape, the story of its construction also inspired novelist William Golding's dark tale simply entitled *The Spire*. The main entrance is to the right of the West Front through a small door via the lovely old cloisters, the largest in England – surprisingly enough given that they were never part of an abbey and built at the same time as the main body of the cathedral. The recommended tourist route then leads into the nave, past probably the oldest working clock in the world, put together in about 1386 and designed without a face just to strike the hours. The nave itself is tall, narrow, and bare, lined with columns of Purbeck marble which were never going to be strong enough to support the spire and required the addition of flying buttresses and strainer arches. The rest of the interior is not as special as some other cathedrals, but highlights include the effigies of William Longespee, half-brother and advisor to King John and the first to be buried in the church, and of the great knight Sir John Cheney, Henry VII's bodyguard who helped defeat Richard III at Bosworth, as well as the base of the shrine of St Osmund complete with holes for the healing of the sick.

The remarkable octagonal **Chapter House**, off the main cloisters, was also built in the mid-13th century, with beautiful 'Geometric' windows, richly carved Purbeck marble columns bursting with flora and fauna and an extraordinary medieval frieze depicting Genesis and Exodus. Also on show is one of the four surviving original copies of the Magna Carta, the foundation stone of the rule of law in the country during the despotic reign of King John.

Almost a mile north of the city centre, **Old Sarum** ① *(EH), Castle Rd, T01722-335398, Apr-Jun, Sep daily 1000-1700, Jul and Aug 0900-1800, Oct 1000-1600, £3.90, concessions £3.50, child (5-15) £2.30*, is a beautifully situated hill fort. Constructed in the Iron Age, it was continuously inhabited until the Middle Ages when the church moved its cathedral into the valley below. Good views from the walks around the walls and the foundations of the original Norman cathedral can still be seen, where William the Conqueror made all the landowners in the country swear allegiance to him.

Cereal thrillers

In the late 1980s and early 1990s, Britain was gripped by Crop Circle fever. Across the south of England, and mostly in Wiltshire, farmers woke to find a series of giant pictograms carved into their fields of cereal crops. What was going on? Many theories were posited as to the origin of these strange designs, ranging from nightly visitations by extra-terrestrial draughtsmen to the more mundane idea of an elaborate hoax. Crop circles are not a recent phenomenon, however. Illustrations showing crop circles date from as long ago as 1647, and crop circles were appearing, in much simpler form, in the early 1970s. But it is only since 1990 that they have taken on their now familiar complex geometric patterns. The Centre for Crop Circle Studies was established in 1990 to give some serious thought to the matter and have revealed some interesting facts. For instance, many of the circles appeared close to sacred sites such as Avebury, Stonehenge, Silbury Hill and Old Sarum, the original site of Salisbury, lending credence to the notion that they could have been formed by ley lines, the powerful current that flows through the earth. The CCCS also discovered that crop yields increased significantly following the appearance of circles, that electronic equipment malfunctioned inside the circles and that people even showed physical side effects such as nausea and dizziness. Crop circles were thrust back into the limelight with the release of the Walt Disney movie, *Signs*, starring Mel Gibson.

North of Salisbury

Stonehenge

ⓘ *(EH), off A344, Amesbury, T01722-343830, mid-Mar to May and Sep to mid-Oct 0930-1800, Jun-Aug 0900-1900, mid-Oct to mid-Mar 0930-1600, £8, child (5-15) £4.80, family £20.80.*
Almost halfway to Exeter from London on the A303, and 7 miles north of Salisbury, stands Britain's most famous and most visited prehistoric monument, Stonehenge. First impressions may be disappointing: big roads rush very close by; the whole place is often mobbed with visitors; walking among the stones is forbidden; and if you've only seen photographs, the standing stone doorways may seem unimpressively small. That said, the informative and entertaining audioguide quickly provokes a sense of wonder at humankind's achievement here during the Bronze Age. The main features of the monument are a circular ditch and bank (a henge), the ancient Heel Stone just outside it (the only naturally shaped stone on site), and in the middle the ruins of a circle of sarsens capped with lintels, a circle of bluestones, a horseshoe of trilithons and the fallen Altar Stone.

Speculation continues as to the true purpose of the stones, broadly agreed to have been erected over the period 3000 BC to 1500 BC. It's sobering to think that the place was probably in use for at least 3000 years, the hub of one of the earliest cultures on the planet. Whether a temple to the sun, an astronomical clock, or gruesome site of ritual sacrifice, its importance can be judged from the fact that many of its stones were somehow transported all the way from the mountains of Wales. Others, including the distinctive 30-ton sarsens and their capping stones, were dragged off the Marlborough Downs some 20 miles to the north. A new **visitor centre** is set to open in October 2013.

When complete, the it will make it possible for the first time to present the fascinating story of Stonehenge on site. An archaeological gallery will feature important objects on loan from local museums and outside will be three Neolithic houses, recreated using extremely rare evidence of domestic buildings from prehistoric England recently unearthed near Stonehenge. A new shuttle service will bridge the one-mile distance between the visitor centre and the stones.

Salisbury Plain
North of Stonehenge stretches Salisbury Plain, much of it an army training ground and off-limits. Walks from the monument itself are pretty limited therefore, although a good overview of its position surrounded by a litter of related earthworks and burial mounds can be found at the crest of **King's Barrow Down**, best reached up a tiny road north just east of the fork in the A303 that pens in Stonehenge with the A344. Just beyond, a minor road south heads down into the Avon Valley and the **Woodfords**, a string of attractive manorial riverside villages crossed by the long-distance **Monarch's Way** footpath. In Middle Woodford, **Heale Gardens** ① *T01722-782504, www.healegarden.co.uk, Feb-Sep Wed-Sat 1000-1700, Sun 1100-1600, £5, child £2.50,* surround a mellow old house (private) with a gorgeous profusion of roses, hedgework and herbaceous borders.

South and west of Salisbury

Down the Avon Valley on the A338, just north of the New Forest and Fordingbridge, is the beautiful Elizabethan **Breamore Manor** ① *Breamore, T01725-512858, www.breamore house.com; Apr Tue and Sun; May-Sep Tue-Thu and Sun; Oct Tue and Sun 1400-1700; £8, child (5-15) £6, family £19,* still lived in by descendants of its early 18th-century purchaser Sir Edward Hulse, physician to Queen Anne and the first two Georges. The interior contains paintings from the 17th- and 18th-century Dutch schools, a unique set of Mexican ethnological paintings and a rare Jacobean carpet. The **Countryside Museum** next door illustrates the lives led in the surrounding 17th-century village and boasts a very unusual Bavarian four-train turret clock from 1575. The village church, detached from the main cluster of buildings, is one of the finest examples of pre-Conquest Saxon architecture in the south.

West of Salisbury, the rivers Wylye, Nadder, and Ebble flow down into the Avon, and each is lined with attractive villages that make good bases for riverside walks. The Ebble is the least developed, overlooked by the Iron Age hill fort of **Clearbury Ring** with great views of the surrounding downs and Salisbury from a thickly overgrown old earthwork on the top of the hill. A mile or so west of Salisbury up the Nadder Valley, **Wilton House** ① *T01722-746714, www.wiltonhouse.com, May-Sep daily 1130-1700 (last admission 1630), £15.50, concessions £12.25, child (5-15) £8, grounds only including adventure playground £6.50, child (5-15) £4.50,* is quite a commercialized stately home, owned by the Earl of Pembroke, but very special inside, with a visitor centre in the Old Riding School, featuring a Victorian laundry and Tudor kitchen. Its most famous room is the Double Cube Room, by Inigo Jones, hung with paintings by Van Dyck and Joshua Reynolds. There's an adventure playground and 21 acres of romantic gardens and the strange Italianate church in town is also worth a look.

A little further west on the A30, past the lovely parkland and church of picturesque Compton Chamberlayne, **Philipps House and Dinton Park** ① *(NT), T01722-538014, house: Mon 1300-1700, Sat 1000-1300, £4; park: daily 0800-dusk, free*, is a fine Palladian mansion containing Regency furniture in a lovely setting in Dinton Park with renovated and restored parkland walks stretching down to a lake.

Other villages in the Nadder Valley worth exploring are **Teffont Magna**, positively the last word in cute thatched villages, near the **Howard's House Hotel** (see page 46) and tiny **Fyfield Bavant**, with a 13th-century church like a little cowshed with a belfry.

A peculiar sight south of the A30 are the **Fovant Badges**, a series of large hill carvings in the strange shapes of regimental badges created by the troops stationed here during the First World War, including the YMCA, the Royal Corps of Signals' figure of Hermes and the London Rifle Brigade. Close by, at **Compton Chamberlayne**, with more acres of attractive parkland, picturesque thatched village and manor, there's also a map of Australia carved into the hill by the many Aussies stationed here.

Salisbury and around listings

For hotel and restaurant price codes, and other relevant information, see pages 9-12.

☺ Where to stay

Salisbury *p39, map p39*

£££ Best Western Red Lion Hotel, 4 Milford St, T01722-323334, www.the-redlion.co.uk. Courtyard hotel in the middle of the city, founded in the 13th century. Reliable restaurant.

£££ Mecure White Hart Salisbury, St John St, T01962-312801, www.mecure.com. Very comfortable 4-star refurbishment of an old townhouse, with real fires, clean rooms and friendly service.

£££ Milford Hall Hotel, 206 Castle St, T01722-417411, www.milfordhallhotel.com. Close to the centre, family-run in an extended Georgian mansion.

£££ The Pembroke Arms, Minster St, Wilton, T01722-743328, www.pembroke arms.co.uk, recently refurbished to make it a luxury boutique with a touch of Indian design amongst the quintessentially English charm, this hotel caters for couples, families and even dogs.

££ The Wardrobe, The Cathedral Close, T01628-825925, www.landmarktrust.org.uk. Unusual find high up in the attics of the Berkshire and Wiltshire Regimental Museum. The windows of this 2nd floor, 2-bedroom apartment frame stunning views of Salisbury Cathedral.

££ Old House, 161 Wilton Rd, T01722-333433, www.theold-house.co.uk. Beamed rooms and friendly family home with charming garden, within walking distance of the city centre.

£ Salisbury YHA, Milford Hill, T01722-3719537, www.yha.org.uk. Good youth hostel set in a 200-year-old villa set in private grounds near Salisbury Cathedral.

North of Salisbury *p43*

£££ Stonehenge Campervans, Foredown House, Winterbourne Stoke, T07747-847763, www.stonehengecampervans.co.uk. Fabulous collection of VW T2 Classic Campervans for hire just 2 miles west of Stonehenge.

South and west of Salisbury *p44*

£££ Howard's House Hotel, Teffont Evias, near Salisbury, T01722-716392, www.howardshousehotel.com. Small and very comfortable country hotel in an idyllic setting with a sweet little garden and boasting a high-quality restaurant that draws in diners from Salisbury and further afield.

£££ Quidhampton Mill B&B, Netherhampton Rd, Quidhampton, T01722-741171, www.quidhamptonmill.co.uk. Featured by *The Sunday Times* as one of the best stays in Wiltshire, this hotel marks a new wave of upmarket B&Bs. 3 rooms – The Cabin, The Bolthole and The Loft – are all in stylish muted colours with fine linens and furnishings. Breakfasts are top notch.

££ The Bell Inn, High St, Wylye, T01985-248338, www.thebellwylye.co.uk. In the shadows of the A303 and A36 but a lovely old pub with comfortable rooms and good local ingredients in its accomplished restaurant.

🍴 Restaurants

Salisbury *p39, map p39*

££ The Asia Restaurant, 90 Fisherton St, T01722-327628. A reliable but quite pricey Indian restaurant.

££ The Haunch of Venison, 1/5 Minster St, T01722-411313, www.haunch-salisbury.com. A famous old pub with a very decent menu of pub grub in the restaurant upstairs.

££ The Lazy Cow, 9-13 St John St, T01722-412028, www.thelazycowsalisbury.co.uk. Old English meets boutique-style steak-and-ale house with plush, trendy rooms.

£ Chef Peking, Fisherton St, T01722-326063. A very tasty and popular Chinese with a lively atmosphere.

🎵 Pubs, bars and clubs

South and west of Salisbury *p44*
The Cartwheel Inn, Whitsbury, T01725-518362, www.cartwheeling.co.uk. A proper country pub with a pool table, garden, good-value pub grub and well-kept beers.
The Cosy Club, College Chambers, 49 New St, T01722-334824, www.cosyclub.co.uk/salisbury. A grade II listed former arts college turned spacious bar with leather arm chairs, retro table and chairs and French chandeliers.
The Crown Inn, Alvediston, T01722-780335, www.thecrown-inn-alvediston.co.uk. A charming thatched 15th-century pub.
Radnor Arms, Nunton, T01722-329722. Offers an interesting modern European menu backed up with some real ales.

🎭 Entertainment

Salisbury *p39, map p39*
A useful leaflet giving details of many concerts throughout the year in the city hall and cathedral as well as churches and schools around the city is also available. See www.musicinsalisbury.org.
Salisbury Arts Centre, Bedwin St, T01722-321744, www.salisburyarts centre.co.uk. Performing and visual arts in a converted church beside parkland.
Salisbury Playhouse, Malthouse Lane, T01722-320333, www.salisburyplay house.com. Well-established haven for touring productions, some warming up for the West End.

🎪 Festivals

Salisbury *p39, map p39*
May/Jun Salisbury Festival, usually last week of May and 1st week of Jun, box office T0845-2419651, www.salisburyfestival.co.uk.

A formidable multi-arts festival with fireworks, outdoor classical concerts, theatre and street shows.

🛍 Shopping

Salisbury *p39, map p39*
Pritchetts, 5 Fish Row, T01722-324346, www.pritchetts.co.uk. Top-quality butcher for mean pork pies and superb sausages.
Reeve the Bakers, 2 Butcher Row, T01722-320367, www.reevethebaker.co.uk. Another place to pick up some delectable picnic materials.

🏔 What to do

Salisbury *p39, map p39*
Old Sarum Flying Club, Old Sarum Airfield, T01722-322525, www.oldsarumairfield.co.uk.
Salisbury Racecourse, Netherhampton, T01722-326461 www.salisburyrace course.co.uk. Horse racing May-Oct at one of the country's oldest and most picturesque courses.
Thruxton Motorsport Centre, Thruxton Circuit, Andover, T01264-882222, www.thruxtonracing.co.uk.

⊖ Transport

Salisbury *p39, map p39*
Car hire Europcar, Fisherton Yard, Fisherton St, T01722-335625; **Thrifty**, Brunel Rd, Churchfields Ind Est, T01722-332323.

Cycle Hire Hayball Cycle Centre, Black Horse Chequer, 26-30 Winchester St, Salisbury T01722-411378, www.hayball.co.uk.

Taxi City Cabs Salisbury, T01722-505055, www.citycabssalisbury.co.uk.

⊕ Directory

Salisbury *p39, map p39*
Hospitals Salisbury District Hospital, Odstock Rd, T01722-336262, www.salisbury.nhs.uk.

Winchester and around

In the middle of Hampshire sits Winchester, a bit mauled by the M3 motorway, but still boasting one of the most noble cathedrals and most beautiful old schools in the country. On its outskirts, beside the river Itchen, the abbey and almshouses at St Cross are probably the best-preserved medieval sight in England. West of Winchester, Romsey is the setting for another great Norman church, while the Test Valley runs north-south, still brimming with trout and attracting some alarmingly well-equipped anglers. East of Winchester, Alresford is an attractive old town, just north of the Meon Valley, with its string of pretty villages. Selborne, just north of Petersfield, has become permanently associated with the great naturalist Gilbert White. South of Winchester, the New Forest is a popular playground for cyclists, walkers and pony-trekkers, as well as being the last extensive stretch of lowland heath to survive in the whole country.

Winchester → *For listings, see pages 56-57.*

Quondam capital of the country under King Alfred the Great, Winchester lost out to London some time in the late Middle Ages. Its royal glory days may be over but it remains a very prosperous city with a distinctive ecclesiastical and scholarly air. The great cathedral's interior is one of the most inspiring in the land and William of Wykeham's public school for boys provided the model for most others. In fact the cathedral with its close, the college and its grounds taken together make up one of the most beautiful medieval complexes in the country, capped by the almost undisturbed peace of St Cross Hospital, still standing quietly close to lovely watermeadows a mile or so to the south, where Keats was inspired to write his *Ode to Autumn*. That said, the city centre itself is only slowly recovering from some seriously ill-advised urban planning; and the destruction of Twyford Down by the M3 caused widespread protest as Areas of Outstanding Natural Beauty and Sites of Special Scientific Interest surrounding the city were brutally destroyed.

Arriving in Winchester

Getting there Winchester is off the M3 at junctions 9-11, about a one-hour drive from London. **National Express** ① *T08717-818178, www.nationalexpress.com*, runs nine coaches a day to Winchester from London Victoria (two hours). Twice hourly direct trains from London Waterloo take about one hour with **South West Trains** ① *T0845-600 0650, www.southwesttrains.co.uk*.

Getting around The centre of Winchester, and its main sights, is easily small enough to walk around, although the walk from train station to the city's outskirts at St Cross would take at least an hour. The network of local buses is run by **Wilts and Dorset Buses** ① *T01722-336855, www.wdbus.co.uk*, and serves areas to the southwest such as Salisbury and Romsey.

Tourist information Winchester TIC ① *Guildhall, High St, T01962-840500, www.visit winchester.co.uk, May-Sep Mon-Sat 1000-1700, Sun 1100-1600, Oct-Apr Mon-Sat 1000-1700.*

Background

The earliest settlement, home of a Celtic people during the fifth century BC, discovered in the Winchester area was on St Catherine's Hill, just south of the modern city, recognizable today by its distinctive 'clump' of trees on the summit. Around 150 BC a tribe of Belgae set up a trading centre near this spot and two centuries later, the Romans turned it into a major regional administrative centre which they called 'Venta Belgarum'. Long after they'd left, shortly after the Dark Ages, when the town is thought by some to have played a part in Arthurian romance as Caer Gwent, Egbert was crowned King of England here in AD 829. More famously, 42 years later, the Anglo-Saxon King Alfred the Great followed in his footsteps, founding a new Minster, establishing the capital here and masterminding resistance to the Vikings. Construction of the cathedral that stands today began just after the Norman Conquest. William the Conqueror was crowned both here and in London. Two hundred years later, Bishop William of Wykeham founded Winchester College. In 1538, Henry VIII's split with Rome mauled the city's monasteries, and by the time his successor 'Bloody' Mary Tudor married the Catholic Philip of Spain, the cathedral had been stripped of its famous shrine to St Swithun, venerable adviser to the Saxon kings.

Less than a century later, Winchester backed the losers in the Civil War, the west window of the cathedral was smashed and Oliver Cromwell's cannon pounded the castle and city into submission. His vantage point to the south is still known as Oliver's Battery. At the Restoration, Charles II took a shine to the place, and planned to build a palace here. It was

Winchester

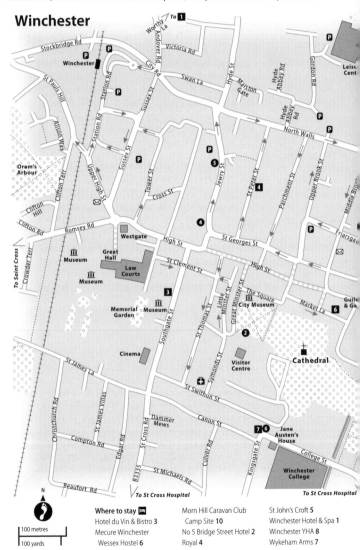

N

100 metres
100 yards

Where to stay 🛏
Hotel du Vin & Bistro **3**
Mecure Winchester
Wessex Hostel **6**

Morn Hill Caravan Club
Camp Site **10**
No 5 Bridge Street Hotel **2**
Royal **4**

St John's Croft **5**
Winchester Hotel & Spa **1**
Winchester YHA **8**
Wykeham Arms **7**

never built though, and after the Glorious Revolution of 1688 the city's royal star faded. Since the 18th century, Winchester has settled into provincial obscurity, and is now a prosperous and polite London satellite.

Restaurants ②
The Black Rat **1**
Brasserie Blanc **5**
Cathedral Refectory **2**
Chesil Rectory **3**
Loch Fyne **4**
Wykeham Arms **6**

Westgate and Great Hall

From the railway station in the northwest of the town, a five-minute walk brings you to the old medieval **Westgate** ① *T01962-848269, Apr-Oct Sat, 1000-1700, Sun 1200-1700; Feb-Mar Sat 1000-1600, Sun 1200-1600, free entry*, at the top of the High Street. Inside there's a brass rubbing centre, and some debtor's graffiti testifying to its use as a prison for more than a century. Better perhaps to hurry on next door to the **Great Hall** ① *T01962-846476, daily 1000-1600, free*, the last remnant of Winchester Castle, impressive nonetheless, where the city's famous Round Table has hung on the wall for more than 500 years. Long associated with King Arthur, he is depicted at its centre in the Tudor costume of the time when it was repainted. Big enough to seat all 24 of his knights, it probably actually originates from sometime in the 13th century. Henry VIII took the Emperor Charles V to see it in 1522. Queen Eleanor's pretty little medieval garden has been reconstructed outside.

Peninsular Barracks

A little further down the High Street, Southgate Street heads off to the right for St Cross Hospital (see below) past the Peninsular Barracks to the **Royal Green Jackets (Rifles) Museum** ① *T01962-828549, www.rgjmuseum.co.uk, Mon-Sat 1000-1700, Sun 1000-1700 (Jul-Sep), £3.50, concessions £2.50, child £2*. Featuring the Rifle Brigade and a diorama of the Battle of Waterloo, it's a real feast for military types young and old.

No less than five military museums are now housed here: the **Light Infantry Museum** ① *T01962-828550, Mon-Sat 1000-1600, Sun 1200-1600, free*, the most modern of them with displays on the collapse of the Berlin Wall and the Gulf War; the **Gurkha Museum** ① *T01962-842832, www.thegurkhamuseum.co.uk, Tue-Sat, 1000-1700, £2, concessions £1*, with exhibits from their homeland in Nepal; the **Royal Hampshire Regiment Museum** ① *Serle's House, Southgate St, T01962-863658, www.serleshouse.co.uk, Tue-Fri 1000-1600, Sat-Sun 1200-1600 (Apr-Oct), free*, with displays on the history of the local militia; and **HorsePower** ① *Romsey Rd, T01962-828541, www.horsepowermuseum.co.uk, Tue-Sat 1000-1245, 1330-1600, Sun 1200-1600, free*, the museum of the King's Royal Hussars.

City Museum

Continuing down the High Street, the **Buttercross** is the local youth hangout with kids sitting vacantly around the heavily restored 15th-century market cross. A passage through the old shops on the right leads into the **Square**, a good approach to the west front of the cathedral. On the Square, the recently re-vamped **City Museum** ① *T01962-863064, www.winchester.gov.uk/heritage, Apr-Oct Mon-Sat 1000-1700, Sun 1200-1700; Nov-Mar Tue-Sat 1000-1600, Sun 1200-1600, free*, tells the story of the city's former national importance entertainingly enough and also includes some of the latest archaeological finds from the site of King Alfred's grave.

Winchester Cathedral

① *T01962-857275, www.winchester-cathedral.org.uk, daily 0830-1700. Services Mon-Sat 0740, 0800 (Thu and Saints' days 1200), 1730, Sun 0800, 1000, 1115, 1530. £7.50, concession £5.50, under 16s free, pay on the day and visit as often as you like for 12 months.*

Even a passing visitor to the city should not fail to look inside Winchester Cathedral. On low ground beside the River Itchen – so low in fact that it began to sink into the marshy ground and was only saved by a brave diver called William Walker pumping concrete into its rotten wooden foundations in the 1920s – the stubby tower may make first impressions disappointing. Approaching the west front from the Square though, the building's scale and grandeur gradually make themselves felt. Inside, the longest medieval nave in Europe never fails to stir the spirit, soaring up to a magnificent vaulted ceiling supported by a splendid march of perpendicular columns. Work was begun on the building 13 years after the Battle of Hastings and completed 14 years later in 1093. Almost two centuries later, the West Front (and main entrance) was remodelled and the nave transformed by Bishop William of Wykeham, founder of St Mary's College (see below) and New College, Oxford. Things to look out for inside include fine statues of Kings James I and Charles I, the grave of Jane Austen, the 12th-century black marble font, extraordinary ancient choir stalls and the marble tomb of William Rufus. Shortly after Rufus – who was possibly assassinated in the New Forest – was buried in the central crossing, the Norman tower collapsed on his grave, many thought as a consequence of his misrule. The east end of the building boasts some of the earliest pure Gothic architecture in the country. Beneath, the crypt – which is still prone to flooding – has become an atmospheric setting for modern sculptor Anthony Gormley's *Sound II*. The Winchester Bible, on display in the library, is a beautiful illuminated 12th-century manuscript, gorgeously gilded and decorated with lapis lazuli from Afghanistan. Guided tours of the cathedral include a trip up the tower, or round the library, triforium (above the nave) and treasury.

To the right of the cathedral's main entrance in the west front a passageway leads beneath flying buttresses into the **Deanery Close**, a very peaceful place near the remains of the old monastery. **Dean Garnier's Garden** is a reconstructed Victorian garden beneath the cathedral walls. At the other end of the close is **Cheyney Court**, a much-photographed half-timbered house where the bishops once held court, next door to **Pilgrim's Hall**, an early 14th-century room with a well-preserved hammer-beam roof. Through the old wall, the city's other surviving medieval gateway, the **Kingsgate** separates the cathedral from the college.

Around College Street

College Street, where Jane Austen lived out the last years of her life, leads off to the left and the impressive main gate of St Mary's College, better known as **Winchester College** ① *T01962-621100, www.winchestercollege.org, guided tours Mon, Wed, Fri and Sat, 1045-1200, 1415-1530, Tue, Thu, 1045-1200, Sun 1415-1530, £6, concessions £5.* One of the oldest (founded 1382), most exclusive and most beautiful schools in the country, guided tours include the dinky little chamber court – a sort of mini Oxbridge college quad for kids – the chapel, quiet cloisters and old dining hall, as well as the school. It's a very correctly proportioned building attributed to Wren, with a funny old picture of the Trusty Servant, a hybrid creature embodying the school's motto: 'Manners maketh man'.

On the other side of College Street are the ruins of the **Old Bishop's Palace** ① *Wolvesey Castle (EH), T02392-378291, Mar-Oct daily 1000-1700, free,* once one of the most important medieval buildings in Europe, where Raleigh was tried and condemned to death, although there's not a huge amount left to see now. Atmospheric nonetheless.

At the end of College Street, a very pleasant walk leads straight on through 'the weirs' of the Itchen to a working watermill, **Winchester City Mill** ① *(NT), Bridge St, T01962-870057, mid-Mar to late Dec 1000-1700, £3.90, child £1.95,* almost back in the middle of town with an impressive rushing water race and island garden. It's also a youth hostel (see page 56). A right turn at the end of College Street heads towards the **watermeadows**, a delightful tract of reedbeds and tiny waterways burgeoning with wildlife. A good mile's walk between these meadows and the school's playing fields along the riverbank finally reaches the other unmissable highlight of a visit to Winchester, **The Hospital of St Cross** ① *St Cross Rd, T01962-878218, Apr-Oct Mon-Sat 0930-1700, Sun 1300-1700; Nov-Mar Mon-Sat 1030-1530, £4, £3.50 concessions, under 13 £2, guided tours bookable in advance in writing.* Founded in 1136, these beautiful old almshouses (the oldest in England) and their wonderful Norman abbey on the riverbank survived the dissolution of the monasteries thanks to being for lay brothers rather than the clergy. Today it must be one of the most perfectly unspoiled medieval places in the country. The current occupants still hand out the Wayfarer's Dole – a bit of bread and beer – to visitors or pilgrims during visiting hours and show people around their adorable church with its chunky round Norman pillars, wealth of zigzag stonework and adjoining Tudor courtyards.

Out of town

Three miles out of Winchester, the **INTECH Science Centre** ① *Morn Hill, T01962-863791, www.intech-uk.com, Mon-Fri 1000-1600, Sat-Sun 1000-1700, £9, concessions £7.50, child (3-16) £6.50, family £27.90, planetarium shows, £2.20 extra,* is an exciting exhibition space with 100 hands-on exhibits that communicate the fundamental principles of science and technology and their applications in industry and the home in a fun and interactive way.

Romsey and the Test Valley

Romsey, 10 miles southwest of Winchester on the A3090, is a pretty little market town most famous for its great Norman nunnery. **Romsey Abbey** ⓘ *T01794-513125, www.romseyabbey.org.uk, Mon-Sat, 0730-1800, Sun, 1100-1800*, was founded by King Alfred's son Edward in 907, demolished by the Danes and rebuilt by the Normans in 1130. Like St Cross Hospital in Winchester, it was lucky to survive the Dissolution, being bought by the citizens of the town for £100. In the reign of William Rufus, the third Abbess Ethelflaeda disguised the Saxon princess Aedgyth as a nun to shield her from the king's desire for a dynastic alliance of the Norman and Saxon crowns. According to local legend, the abbess was also in the habit of reciting her psalms naked by moonlight in the river Test. Today the church is crowded around by the town but remains one of the grandest set-pieces of Norman architecture in the country.

In the market place of Romsey stands a statue of Lord Palmerston, the mid-19th-century prime minister who changed from Tory to Whig and on his deathbed said "Die, my dear Doctor, that's the last thing I shall do!" He lived at **Broadlands** ⓘ *T01794-505022, www.broadlandsestates.co.uk, Jul-Aug Mon-Fri 1300-1730, £8, child (5-16) £4*, the grand 18th-century stately home with landscaped grounds sloping down to the river. Later it became the home of Lord Louis Mountbatten, last Viceroy and first Governor General of India, and the stable-block houses an exhibition on his life's achievements and naval exploits.

Five miles north of Romsey on the A3057 is **Mottisfont Abbey** ⓘ *(NT), T01794-340757, grounds, Mar-Oct, 1100-1700 (rose garden 1000-1700)*, the remains of a 12th-century priory on the River Test with an 18th-century house built round it, featuring Rex Whistler's trompe-l'oeil drawing room, a 19th- and 20th-century art collection and peaceful gardens famous for their old-fashioned rose collection.

Six miles further north, the same road following the course of the River Test arrives in **Stockbridge** (9 miles west of Winchester). A picturesque one-street town lined with antique shops and twee tearooms, this is the trout fly-fisherman's favourite Hampshire residence and a popular staging post on the long-distance walk the **Test Way**, 71 miles from Eling Wharf to Inkpen Beacon.

Danebury Vineyard ⓘ *3 miles northwest of the town, T01264-781851, www.danebury.com*, is a 6-acre vineyard in the grounds of Danebury House, with tastings and food in a grand south-facing setting. Close by is **Danebury Hill Fort**, one of the south's more spectacular Iron Age hill forts. The history of the fort can be explored in **Andover**, 7 miles north of Stockbridge, at the **Museum of the Iron Age** ⓘ *6 Church Close, Andover, T0845-603 5635, Tue-Fri 1000-1700, Sat 1000-1600, free*. Just beyond Danebury, in Middle Wallop, the **Museum of Army Flying** ⓘ *T01264-784421, www.armyflying.com, daily 1000-1630, £9, child (5-16) £6.50*, is a pretty impressive example of its type, with a unique collection of military gliders and more than 35 other flying machines, from biplanes to choppers. It also includes a popular interactive science education gallery for kids called Explorer's World, featuring a camera obscura with views over the surrounding countryside that adults might well enjoy too.

East of Winchester → *For listings, see pages 56-57.*

With the Itchen Valley north and south of Winchester pretty much destroyed by the M3, it's refreshing to escape east on the B2177 to the uncommercialized old town of Bishops Waltham. On the way, five miles south east of Winchester, is **Marwell Zoo** ① *Colden Common, near Winchester, T01962-777407, www.marwell.org.uk, Apr-Nov daily 1000-1700, Dec-Mar daily 1000-1600, £18, concessions £15.50, child £14.* Admission may be expensive but then there are a surprising number of rare and endangered species being well looked after here. As well as roomy enclosures for the likes of lemurs, penguins and gazelles on the 100-acre site, there are also plenty of sideshow activities for kids.

Bishops Waltham, about 9 miles southeast of Winchester, was once wholly owned by the Bishops of Winchester. The attractive Georgian town on the River Hamble now clusters around the evocative remains of their **palace** ① *(EH), T0870-3331181, May-Sep daily 1000-1700, free,* built by Bishop Henry of Blois in the Middle Ages, with moated grounds, ruined great hall and chapel. It's how Oxbridge colleges might have looked if abandoned after the Dissolution.

Slightly further east, the A32 winds up from Fareham and Gosport through the **Meon Valley**, passing through a string of well-to-do and very well-kept towns and villages such as Droxford, Warnford and West Meon. Nearby, **Old Winchester Hill**, just to the east, is another Iron Age hill fort worth a climb, with excellent views towards the sea and over the surrounding downs.

New Alresford, 7 miles east of Winchester on the A31, is an attractive old market town (christened 'new' in the 13th century) with a good variety of interesting shops and pubs, as well as the terminus of the **Mid-Hants Watercress Line** ① *railway station, Alresford, T01962-733810, www.watercressline.co.uk.* A popular outing for families not wholly obsessed with steam because its 10-mile journey from Alresford to Alton via Ropley, Medstead and Four Marks (the highest station in southern England) runs through delightful countryside. The steam trains link up with the national rail network at Alton.

Not far from Alresford, the formal and informal hillside gardens around a fine Georgian house at **Hinton Ampner** ① *(NT), Bramdean, Alfresford, T01962-771305; house Feb-Oct daily 1100-1700, Nov Sat-Wed 1100-1630; gardens Feb-Oct daily 1000-1700, Nov Sat-Wed 1100-1700; £8.50, child £4.10,* are a joy to behold in season and have wonderful views.

Selborne, 5 miles southwest of Alton, is a quaint little village nestling beneath the Hangar. This steep wood was made famous by the writer **Gilbert White** whose *Natural History of Selborne* published in 1789 set the standard for many early ecologists. His **house** ① *The Wakes, Selborne, Alton, T01420-511275, www.gilbertwhiteshouse.org.uk, Jan to mid-Feb Fri-Sun 1030-1630; mid-Feb to Mar Tue-Sun 1030-1630; Apr-Oct Tue-Sun 1030-1715; Nov-late Dec Tue-Sun 1030-1630, £8.50, concessions £7.50, under-16s £3,* and an original manuscript, have been preserved, and his garden restored to its 18th-century state. On the upper floors of the house, the **Oates Museum** honours the memory of Captain Oates, who sacrificed his life for his fellows on Scott's ill-fated expedition to the Antarctic by leaving the tent during a blizzard saying "I am just going outside and may be some time."

Winchester and around listings

For hotel and restaurant price codes, and other relevant information, see pages 9-12.

⊙ Where to stay

Winchester *p49, map p50*

££££ Mecure Winchester Wessex Hotel, Paternoster Row, T01962-312800, www.mecure.com. The smart option (if a touch impersonal) in an excellent position on the close, many rooms with cathedral views.

£££ Hotel du Vin and Bistro, 14 Southgate St, T01962-841414, www.hotelduvin.com. Stylish and comfortable hotel with pleasantly informal service and top-notch brasserie. Great views of the cathedral's west front and over Winchester from the top rooms.

£££ Winchester Hotel & Spa, Worthy Lane, T01962-709988, www.the winchesterhotel.co.uk. Conveniently located just across from the station, the recently refurbished hotel is comfortable and smart, if a tiny bit soulless, with a lovely new spa.

£££ Winchester Royal Hotel, St Peter St, T0844-8559141, www.akkeronhotels.com. Renovated old hotel of great character with beautiful garden and famous conservatory dining room.

£££ Wykeham Arms, 75 Kingsgate St, T01962-853834, www.wykehamarms winchester.co.uk. Comfortable, stylish rooms in one of the best pubs in the city, right by the college and Cathedral Close.

£££-££ No 5 Bridge Street Hotel, 5 Bridge St, T01962-863838, www.no5bridgestreet. co.uk. Atmospheric bar and restaurant for great wine and tapas with 6 comfy, modern rooms.

££ Mrs Fetherston-Dilke, 29 Christchurch Rd, T01962-868661, www.bedbreakfast winchester.co.uk. Beautiful Regency-style family house, out of centre but close to St Cross.

££ St John's Croft, St John's St, T01962-859976, www.st-johns-croft.co.uk. Period house B&B on St Giles Hill with high ceilings, 10-min walk from the cathedral.

£ Winchester YHA, 1 Water Lane, T01962-853723, www.yha.org.uk. Worth booking well in advance for it's prime position in National Trust City Mill on the Itchen, at the foot of the High St and Broadway. 31 beds in 1-, 4-, 9- and 18-bedded rooms.

Camping

£ Morn Hill Cararvan Club Site, Morn Hill, 3 miles east of the city centre, off the A31, T01962-869877. Open Apr-Oct.

West of Winchester *p54*

£££ The Greyhound Inn, 31 High St, Stockbridge, T01264-810833. Smart restaurant with 4 comfortable rooms, typically Stockbridge.

£££ Lainston Country House Hotel, Woodman Lane, Sparsholt, T01962-776088, www.lainstonhouse.com. Posh country-house hotel in the heart of Winchester where George Bush stayed whilst in town. There's a sense of grandeur with country pursuits such as falconry and fishing.

££ The Grosvenor Hotel High St, Stockbridge, T01264-810606, www.thegrosvenor-hotel.com. Home of the famous Houghton Fishing Club, hence very busy in May, but a reasonably good 'country house' bet in the middle of town.

East of Winchester *p55*

££ Dean Farm, Kilmeston, near Alresford, T01962-771286, www.warrdeanfarm.co.uk. An 18th-century farmhouse B&B on the edge of the Hampshire Downs.

Self-catering

Forest Holidays, Blackwood Forest, Micheldever, T0845-130 8223, www.forest holidays.co.uk. Contemporary, glass-fronted cabins on Forestry Commission land sleep between 2 and 10, some with woodburning stoves and private hot tubs.

🍴 Restaurants

Winchester *p49, map p50*

£££ The Bistro in the **Hotel du Vin** (see page 56) has become easily one of the best dining options in the city, and needn't break the bank with its liberal attitude to combining choices from the simple Frenchified menu.

£££ The Black Rat, 88 Chesil St, T01962-844465, www.theblackrat.co.uk. High-quality modern British food in a stylish converted pub.

£££ Brasserie Blanc, 19-20 Jewry St, T01962-810870, www.brasserieblanc.com. Converted Georgian shops now house this popular French-style brasserie.

£££ Chesil Rectory, Chesil St, T01962-851555, www.chesilrectory.co.uk. Smart cuisine using seasonal, local produce in one of the oldest buildings in the city.

££ Cathedral Refectory, Inner Close, T01962-857258, www.winchester-cathedral.org.uk. Reasonably priced fresh local ingredients confidently put together in the shadow of the cathedral with tables outside.

££ Loch Fyne, 18 Jewry St, T01962-872930, www.lochfyne-restaurants.com. One of the very fresh fish chain from Scotland in a renovated 16th-century building.

££ Wykeham Arms, 75 Kingsgate St, T01962-853834, www.wkyehamarms winchester.co.uk. Very popular top-quality old pub with wholesome traditional food and welcoming scholarly atmosphere.

🍷 Pubs, bars and clubs

East of Winchester *p55*
Brushmakers Arms, 2 Shoe Lane, Upham, Near Bishops Waltham, T01489-860231, www.brushmakers-arms.co.uk. Real ale free house with outside seating and reliable food.
The Globe on the Lake, The Soke, Alresford, T01962-733118. Ambitious menu on the shores of Old Alresford pond with large waterside garden and real ales.
Harrow Inn, Steep, Petersfield, T01730-262685, www.harrow-inn.co.uk. Traditional old country pub, beers through the hatch and big fireplace in an attractive village.
Sun Inn, Bentworth, near Alton, T01420-562338, www.thesuninnbentworth.co.uk. Cosy log-fired pub hidden down a country lane with good real ales and tables outside.
White Horse Inn (the 'Pub with No Name'), Priors Dean, near Petersfield, T01420-588387, www.thepubwithnoname.co.uk. Perched up on the downs, good food and own-brew beers in a popular pub celebrated by the poet Edward Thomas. Serves fine home-made pies in colourful flower-filled courtyard.

✺ Festivals

Winchester *p49, map p50*
Jul Winchester Hat Fair, 5a Jewry St, T01962-840440, www.hatfair.co.uk. Usually in early Jul, is the longest running festival of street theatre in Britain. Over 40 companies from all over the world take part in the festival.

🔺 What to do

Winchester *p49, map p50*
Leisure centres
River Park Leisure Centre, Gordon Rd, Winchester, T01962-848700, www.dcleisure centres.co.uk/centres/river-park-leisure-centre. Swimming pool, 'twister' flume ride, sauna, steam rooms, fitness suites.

Walking
Long distance walks Pilgrim's Trail: 28 miles from Winchester to Portsmouth. **St Swithun's Way**: 43 miles from Winchester to Farnham. **South Downs Way**: 100 miles from Winchester to Eastbourne. **Clarendon Way**: 26 miles from Winchester to Salisbury.

⊙ Directory

Winchester *p49, map p50*
Hospitals Royal Hampshire County Hospital, Romsey Rd, T01962-863535, www.hampshire hospitals.nhs.uk/contact-us/royal-hampshire-county-hospital/index.html. **Internet** The Byte, 10 Parchment St, T01962-83235.

New Forest

Neither new, nor really a forest, the New Forest remains without doubt one of the most individual stretches of countryside in the south of England. Ever since William the Conqueror made it his personal hunting ground almost a thousand years ago, the forest has been a playground for Londoners. Much of the area could now more aptly be described as open heathland, one of the most ecologically important sites in lowland Britain, although the wooded parts do contain a notable variety of trees. The Norman king's son and successor, William Rufus, was shot by an arrow in mysterious circumstances while out hunting, and the Rufus Stone – an unremarkable 18th-century boulder near Fordingbridge – marks the spot. Deer do still abound, but their stocky little four-legged cousins, the New Forest ponies, are much more high profile around here. Amiable enough when not with foal, these peaceable free-range grazers give the area its special character. The historic towns and villages dotted about heave with visitors during summer, but it's always possible to get away from them all by taking a walk in the woods.

Arriving in the New Forest

Getting there The New Forest stretches away to the coast south of the M3/M27/A31 between Southampton and Ringwood, most of it accessible in about two hours from London. A fairly comprehensive network of local buses is run by **Wilts and Dorset Bus** ① *T01202-673555, www.wdbus.co.uk*, open-topped in summer. By train, Brockenhurst is the main station in the forest, with over 100 trains stopping there every day. **Southwest Trains** ① *T08457-484950, www.southwesttrains.co.uk*, links Brockenhurst, New Milton and Christchurch with London Waterloo, Basingstoke, Winchester, Southampton, Bournemouth, Poole and Weymouth. **Cross Country Trains** ① *T08457-484950, www.cross countrytrains.co.uk*, connect with reading, Oxford, Banbury, Coventry, Birmingham and the north. Beaulieu Road is a station in the middle of nowhere between Lyndhurst and Beaulieu, a good starting point for walks.

Getting around The New Forest is best explored on foot, pony or by bike. Local buses require some patience but connect the main towns and villages during the main part of the day, except on Sundays.

Tourist information The **New Forest Visitor and Information Centre** ① *Lyndhurst, T023-8028 2269, www.thenewforest.co.uk, daily 1000-1700*, is an efficient, friendly and well-stocked information centre with accommodation booking service. **Fordingbridge Information Office** ① *Kings Yard, Salisbury St, T01425-654560, Nov-Mar, Mon, Wed and Fri 1000-1600, Apr-Oct, Mon-Fri 1000-1600, Sat 1000-1300*. **The Forestry Commission** ① *T0117-906 6000, www.forestry.gov.uk*, provides details of guided walks and camping facilities within the forest.

Places in the New Forest

Lyndhurst

Lyndhurst, 5 miles south of Junction 1 of the M27, is the capital of the New Forest, a quaint and surprisingly unspoiled little town with a single main street. The church contains some good pre-Raphaelite stained glass. Close by, the old **Queen's House** ① *T023-8028 3134*, and **Verderer's Hall** are the antique setting for the Verderer's Court, which sits on the third Monday of every month except August and December. This occasionally lively anachronism settles disputes over the forest dwellers' rights to peculiarities like turbary (cutting firewood), marl (digging for lime) and pannage (letting their pigs out to graze). In the main car park of the town, the place to find out about the area's special status and much more is the **New Forest Visitor and Information Centre** (see page 59), where there's also a mildly diverting exhibition on the local history.

    The **New Forest Wildlife Park** ① *Deerleap Lane, Longdown, Ashurst, T023-8029 2408, www.newforestwildlifepark.co.uk, spring/summer daily 1000-1730, autumn/winter daily 1000-dusk, £10.50, child (3-16) £7.50, under-3s free*, is set in 25 acres of ancient woodland on the edge of the New Forest. The park is home to Europe's largest collection of multi-specied otters, owls and other indigenous wildlife. The tree-lined walks make the most of the park's location, and there's a tearoom to relax in afterwards.

Walks in the New Forest

- **Bolderwood Green**: 4-mile circle. Start: Bolderwood Grounds carpark, on the minor road from Emery Down to Linwood. A woodland walk that includes a labelled arboretum, deer sanctuary and ancient Douglas firs. OS Maps: Outdoor Leisure 22.

- **Portuguese Fireplace**: 5-mile circle. Start: Millyford Bridge, on the road from Emery Down to Linwood. An easy walk south from a memorial to Portuguese allies through the woods to the Knightwood Oak. OS Maps: Outdoor Leisure 22.

- **Brock Hill**: 3-mile circle. Start: Rhinefield Ornamental Drive. A walk up an avenue of the oldest and tallest pine trees in the forest, past its first enclosure at Vinney Ridge, to a clump of ancient oaks and beeches. OS Maps: Outdoor Leisure 22.

- **Beaulieu**: 4 miles there and back. Start: Beaulieu village. A walk down the Beaulieu river to Buckler's Hard and back along the Solent Way. OS Maps: Outdoor Leisure 22.

- **Queens Bower**: 1 mile there and back. Start: Ober Corner, west of Brockenhurst. An open and marshland stroll to the confluence of the Lymington and Ober rivers near an old hunting lodge. OS Maps: Outdoor Leisure 22.

Beaulieu and around

From Lyndhurst, three roads fan out across the forest. The most attractive (and often a slow-moving traffic jam in high season) is the B3056 to **Beaulieu**, past Beaulieu Road station. Beaulieu is indeed a 'beautiful place', its ancient **abbey** brooding at the head of the river estuary, across the water from the peaceful old estate village. Most of the cars are quite likely to be heading for Lord Montagu's **National Motor Museum** ⓘ *T01590-612345, www.beaulieu.co.uk, Jun-Sep daily 1000-1800, Oct-May 1000-1700, £20, child (13-17) £12, child (5-12) £9.95*, in the grounds of his family's old house, once the gatehouse of the abbey. The museum was started to indulge Montagu's own interests, and now there are more than 250 vehicles to see, including the recordbreaker Bluebird, and 'Bond in Motion', the world's largest official collection of James Bond vehicles. Almost as much a theme park as a museum, you can take a stroll down a 1930s street and race through time in a space-age pod. In the house itself are Victorian costumed guides and there's an exhibition on monastic life at the Domus of Beaulieu Abbey, dating from 1204. Or try a ride on the monorail. The high price of admission is usually justified, especially during one of the regular motoring club events at weekends.

From Beaulieu a narrow road winds for 3 miles down the estuary to **Buckler's Hard** ⓘ *T01590-616203, www.bucklershard.co.uk, Apr-Sep daily 1030-1730, Oct-Mar daily 1000-1630, £4.50, child £2.50*, built from scratch in the 18th century by the Montagu family as a speculative sugar harbour and then used as a naval dockyard for the construction of several of Nelson's ships of the line. The single grassy street slopes down to the riverside, often very crowded in summer but well worth an overnight stay to enjoy the tranquility of the place once all the trippers have gone home. Now it's also a popular yachting centre with a couple of museums on the living quarters and activity in the shipyard during its heyday.

Lymington and around

From Buckler's Hard the long-distance footpath the **Solent Way** heads along one of the few undeveloped stretches of forest coastline, passing the impressive ruins of one of the largest medieval tithe barns in England at St Leonard's Grange, to Lymington, 7 miles west. A yachting centre to rival Cowes further up the Solent, Lymington is the leaping off point for Yarmouth on the Isle of Wight and scarcely preserves its dignity under the onslaught of braying boaties and their flashy fibreglass toys. The little harbour area throngs with holidaymakers looking over the tackle and cramming into dinky alleyways lined with gift shops, tearooms and nautical nick-nacks. Sloping uphill, the town's Georgian High Street is also worth a look. The **St Barbe Museum and Art Gallery** ① *New St, T01590-676969, www.stbarbe-museum.org.uk, Mon-Sat 1000-1600, £4, child (5-16) £2, under 5s free*, is a small local history museum and puts on temporary exhibitions of contemporary artists.

Keyhaven, 4 miles west of Lymington, is a small village at the foot of a long shingle spit sheltering a tidal nature reserve. At the tip of the spit, **Hurst Castle** ① *(EH), T01590-642344, www.hurstcastle.co.uk, Apr-Sep daily 1030-1730, Oct daily 1030-1600, Nov-Mar weekends only 1030-1600, £4.50, child £2.50*, is another of Henry VIII's coastal fortifications, extended massively by the Victorians. Charles I was held prisoner here before being transferred to Carisbrooke. You can take a boat through the salt marsh nature reserve from Keyhaven to the grim-looking place, the nearest point to the Isle of Wight, and enjoy the amazing views and warren of atmospheric rooms. Alternatively, you can walk out to the castle along the calf-stretching shingle beach.

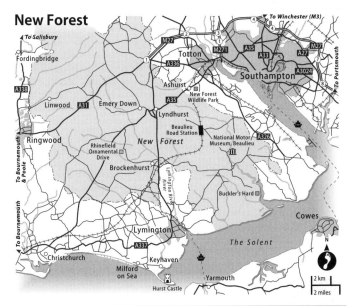

New Forest

On the coast west of Keyhaven, **Milford-on-Sea** is one of the area's prettier seaside towns, with a village green and good swimming beach. **Christchurch**, 8 miles further west, sits at the mouth of the River Avon on the outskirts of Bournemouth. It's managed to resist being swamped by that Victorian holidaymakers' Mecca though, and its central marketplace is still recognizably medieval. The large **priory church** (the longest parish church in the country) dates from that time and is decorated inside with some of the most extraordinary stone carving in the south. The church's north transept is described by church-reviewer Simon Jenkins as "one of the most spectacular works of Norman design in England". High praise for such an under-visited church, now sadly hemmed in by the banal retirement homes stretching along the coast.

From Christchurch, the B3347 winds for 7 miles up the Avon Valley to **Ringwood**, a forest town whose character has almost been obliterated by the A31 and A348 coming up from Bournemouth. Six miles north on the A338, **Fordingbridge** is a much more attractive old town on the banks of the river. West of Fordingbridge can be found one of the largest roman villas ever excavated in the country: **Rockbourne Roman Villa** ① *T0845-6035635, www3.hants.gov.uk/rockbourne-roman-villa, Apr-Sep Thu, Fri, Sun 1100-1600, £3.20, child (5-15) £2.10*. Relatively recently discovered, it spanned several of the first few centuries AD. There's an informative display on Roman life here, followed by a well-signposted look around the site itself. Highlights include the exposed underfloor heating of the two bath houses from AD 150 and the mosaic, still largely intact, on the dining room floor.

New Forest listings

For hotel and restaurant price codes, and other relevant information, see pages 9-12.

🛏 Where to stay

New Forest *p58*

££££ Chewton Glen, New Milton, T01425-275341, www.chewtonglen.com. Frequently voted one of the best 5-star hotels in England, this expensive hotels delivers on all fronts with 70 beautiful suites including 12 new treehouse suites, a renowned restaurant and over 700 wines, an award-winning spa and a vast range of activities from golf to Apache buggy racing. It's also very family friendly.

££££ Limewood, Beaulieu Rd, Lyndhurst, T02380-287177, www.limewoodhotel.co.uk. Bringing a breath of fresh air to 5-star luxury in the New Forest, **Limewood** is all about creating a fabulous world that you never want to leave. Top chef, Angela Harnett, heads up the kitchens where there's a big emphasis on locally sourced, foraged and cured food. Rooms have a magical forest feel whilst being modern and sophisticated. The spa is one of the best in the UK and you can even do yoga on the roof in a herb garden.

££££ Master Builder's House Hotel, Buckler's Hard, Beaulieu, T0844-8153399, www.themasterbuilders.co.uk. Its location on the banks of the Beaulieu River, at the end of the single grassy street that is Buckler's Hard, makes the **Master Builder's House Hotel** somewhere rather special, with traditional English country rooms.

£££ The Beach House (formerly **Westover Hall**), Park Lane, Milford-on-Sea, T01590-643044, www.beachhousemilfordonsea.co.uk. A much needed makeover has brought light and energy to this charming Victorian millionaire's seaside villa, with individual rooms of great character, many with sea views as well as a beautiful restaurant, bar and garden.

£££ The Mill at Gordleton, Silver St, near Lymington, T01590-682219, www.themillatgordleton.co.uk. Attractive pub and restaurant hotel with twee water gardens and highly rated restaurant.

£££ The Pig, Beaulieu Rd, Brockenhurst, T01590-622354, www.thepighotel.com. Little sister hotel to **Limewood**, **The Pig**'s heart and soul is with food. Everything here is about the walled garden, foraging and locally sourced food. Garden to plate is the motto here. All 26 rooms are beautifully shabby chic. Guests can't fail to unwind here and there's even a spa treatment room in the potting shed.

£££ Rhinefield House Hotel, Rhinefield Rd, Brockenhurst, T0845-072 7516, www.handpickedhotels.co.uk. Stunning Gothic stone mansion set in 40 acres of gardens. There's a swimming pool, tennis courts and plenty of pampering.

£££ Stanwell House Boutique Hotel, High St, Lymington, T0844-704 6820, www.stanwellhousehotel.co.uk. Right on the town's main drag, funky restaurant and bar with garden out back and non-chintzy rooms.

££ Alderholt Mill, Sandelheath Rd, Fordingbridge, T01425-653130, www.alderholtmill.co.uk. A working watermill offering B&B, with a lovely back garden. Very good value.

££ Carrington Farmhouse, 22 Keyhaven Rd, Milford-on-Sea, T01590-641949. A 16th-century cottage B&B close to Keyhaven ferry.

££ Compasses Inn, Damerham, near Fordingbridge, T01725-518231, www.compassesinndamerham.co.uk. Pleasant rooms in an attractive pub on the western fringe of the forest, offering reasonable grub.

£ Burley YHA, Cott La, Burley, near Ringwood, T0800-019 5465, www.yha.org.uk/school-trips/hostel/burley. A former family house with 36 beds in 1-, 4-,

6- and 10-bedded rooms, next to the **White Buck Inn**. Quite hard to reach without a car.

🍴 Restaurants

New Forest *p58*

£££ The Jetty Restaurant, Bar & Terrace, 95 Mudeford, Christchurch, T01202-400950, www.rhodes-south.co.uk. Peaceful water's edge dining overlooking Mudeford Quay with local fish dishes.

£££ Limewood and **The Pig** (see Sleeping). Both top restaurants within a hotel setting, with a focus on locally sourced food.

£££ Terravina, 174 Woodlands Rd, Woodlands, Ashurst, T02380-293784, www.hotelterravina.co.uk. Chic restaurant with rooms with open kitchen and alfresco dining in summer. Good for Sun lunch with meat cooked in a wood-burning stove.

£££ Vetiver Restaurant, Chewton Glen, New Milton, T01425-275341, www.chewtonglen.com/restaurant. High-class cooking overlooking the exclusive hotel grounds, good for a special occasion.

££ East End Arms, Lymington Rd, East End, T01590-626223, www.eastendarms.co.uk. Pleasant New Forest gastropub.

££ Egan's Restaurant, 24 Gosport St, Lymington, T01590-676165, www.egans lymington.co.uk. Cheerfully decorated fresh fish restaurant just off the High St in Lymington.

££ The Ship Inn, The Quay, Lymington, T01590-676903, www.theshiplymington. co.uk. Gourmet pub right on the quayside.

£ Beach House Café, Mudeford Sandspit, T01202-423474, www.beachhousecafe.co.uk. Unpretentious dog-and-child-friendly café/restaurant near the jetty. Packed in summer with families enjoying *moules frites* alfresco.

🍸 Pubs, bars and clubs

New Forest *p58*

The Chequers Inn, Lower Woodside, Lymington, T01590-673415, www.chequersinnlymington.com. Country pub with barbecue, very popular with the hearty boating community.

Gun Inn, Keyhaven, T01590-642391, www.theguninn.com. Basic inexpensive food and good beer in a cheery local boozer near the ferry to Hurst Castle and Isle of Wight.

New Forest Inn, Emery Down, T02380-284690, www.thenewforestinn.co.uk. Large back garden in a picturesque village at the heart of the forest with standard pub food. Also offers B&B accommodation.

Red Lion, Ropehill, Boldre, T01590-673177, www.theredlionboldre.co.uk/node/23. Flower-bedecked boozer on the edge of the forest with beamed rooms and bar food.

Royal Oak, North Gorley, T01425-652244, www.royaloakgorley.com. A thatched country pub in picturesque surroundings on the western edge of the forest, where you can sit and watch the ducks on the pond while supping your pint from the local Ringwood Brewery. Good-value pub grub too.

🛍 Shopping

New Forest *p58*

Branksome China Works, Shaftesbury St, Fordingbridge, T01425-652010, www.branks omechina.co.uk. Hand-glazed and crafted fine porcelain crockery with tours of the factory.

Lymington Antiques Centre, 76 High St, T01590-670934. A hotbed of local antique collecting activity.

🏞 What to do

New Forest *p58*
Boating

Puffin Cruises, Lymington, T07850-947618, www.puffincruiseslymington.com. Boat trips from Lymington Town Quay to Yarmouth and the Isle of Wight. Sea-fishing trips from Keyhaven: 6- to 8-hr deep-sea trips, 3-hr mackerel trips.

Horse riding

For a comprehensive list of riding schools in the area visit www.thenewforest.co.uk/activities/stables.aspx.

Burley Villa School of Riding, near New Milton, T01425-610278, www.burley villa.co.uk. For Western-style riding.

Burley Wagonette Rides, Burley, T07786-371843, www.wagonrides.co.uk. Old-fashioned horse and carriage rides. 20 mins to 1 hr 30 mins, £5-16, child £3-8. Easter-Oct daily 1100-1600.

New Park Manor Stables, New Park, Lyndhurst Rd, Brockenhurst, T01590-623919. Another reputable residential riding school and stables, marginally less expensive than most.

Leisure centres

Calshot Activities Centre, Calshot Spit, Fawley, New Forest, T023-8089 2077, www.hants.gov.uk/calshot. One of the largest activity centres in Britain in an extraordinary position next to Calshot Castle on the spit. Facilities include 3 ski slopes, a climbing wall, indoor velodrome and watersports.

New Forest Waterpark, Ringwood Rd, Fordingbridge, T01425-656868, www.newforestwaterpark.co.uk. Fabulous watermark set in 50 acres of countryside with a wide range of watersports available including waterskiing, wakeboarding, kayaking, paddleboarding and inflatable rides. Camping available on site too.

Walking

Long-distance walks Solent Way: Milford-on-Sea to Emsworth (60 miles), a long-distance coastal footpath.

😑 Transport

New Forest *p58*

Cycle

AA Bike Hire, Lyndhurst, Fernglen, T02380-283349, www.aabikehirenewforest.co.uk; **Adventure Cycles**, 97 Station Rd, New Milton, T01425-615960; **Beaulieu**, T01590-611029. **Cyclexperience**, Island Shop, 2-4 Brookley Rd, Brockenhurst, T01590-624204, www.cyclex.co.uk; **Forest Leisure Cycling**, Village Centre Burley, T01425-403584, www.forestleisurecycling.co.uk, reliably good cycle hire in the heart of the New Forest.

Taxi

Marchwood Motorways Taxi Service, T02380-659843, www.marchwood motorwaytaxis.co.uk.

Isle of Wight

From the moment you cross the Solent, the Isle of Wight feels like a proper holiday adventure. Just 23 by 13 miles, the 'sunshine isle' has always had a quirky charm all of its own. It's often observed that it represents the south of England in miniature. Geologically speaking that's certainly accurate, the heavy clay in the north giving away to a pair of downland chalk ridges, one of them breaking up in quite spectacular style in the sea to the west at the Needles. And there's more than a touch of little England about the place as a whole, with its old Norman castle, high-security prisons and social problems besetting the capital Newport in the middle, busy harbours in the north and tidy manor house villages snuggled up in the rolling hills inland. The east coast, best served by public transport, is where the majority of trippers head, in the retirement and seaside entertainment resorts of Sandown, Shanklin and Ventnor. The south has the most beautiful coastline, while the north can boast one of the epicentres of world yachting at Cowes. The island has carved out a niche for itself as a great music festival venue hosting the Isle of Wight Festival in mid-June and Bestival in early September. However cycling, walking, bucket-and-spade and boating holidays are what the Isle of Wight does best. Nothing fancy, not that cheap, even a bit tired perhaps, but all jolly good clean fun.

Arriving on the Isle of Wight

Getting there Car ferries leave the mainland for the Isle of Wight from Southampton, Portsmouth and Lymington. **Wightlink** ① *T0871-3761000, www.wightlink.co.uk*, runs ferries from Portsmouth to Ryde (high-speed passenger service), taking 15 minutes, every 30 minutes; Portsmouth to Fishbourne (car and passenger service), taking 40 minutes, every 30 minutes; and Lymington to Yarmouth (car and passenger service), taking 30 minutes, every 30 minutes. **Red Funnel** ① *T0845-330 8889, www.redfunnel.co.uk*, runs passenger/ vehicle services to East Cowes from Southampton every 50 minutes; while the Red Jet Hi-Speed passenger service runs to West Cowes from Southampton every 30 minutes. **Hovertravel** ① *T01983-811000, www.hovertravel.co.uk*, runs passenger services between Ryde Esplanade and Southsea in under 10 minutes; there is a frequent service running seven days a week. For day-tripping foot passengers, the cheapest and most charming option from late May to September is the tiny **Keyhaven to Yarmouth Ferry** ① *www.thereandwhere.com/where/keyhaven%20ferry*, which takes about 40 minutes leaving Keyhaven at 0915, 1030, 1230, 1630 and returning from Yarmouth at 1000, 1130, 1330, 1530, 1715. Bicycles can be taken on board. For water taxis contact T07766-310751 or T07802-503678.

Getting around A car or bicycle are easily the best ways of reaching some of the island's more impressive beauty spots. Roads are well signposted but some are narrow so drive carefully. Cycling, especially, is a joy out of season on the smaller roads that criss-cross the southwest of the island around Godshill, Wroxall and Brading, or from Yarmouth to the south coast. In summer, traffic usually finds its way into even the most remote corners of the island.

The east coast resorts of Ryde, Sandown, Shanklin and Ventnor are fairly well served by public transport; buses also serve the west of the island but less frequently. Island-wide bus services are run by **Southern Vectis** ① *T0871-200 2233, www.islandbuses.info*, see Transport, page 79, for details of routes. The useful **Island Coaster** bus runs March-September from Ryde following the coast clockwise to Yarmouth. **Rover Tickets** allow unlimited travel on any Southern Vectis bus route during the day, including open-top bus rides. A 24-hour ticket costs £10 (concessions/child £5).

Island Line ① *www.southwesttrains.co.uk/island-line.aspx*, operates trains from Ryde Pier to Shanklin, via Ryde Esplanade, Brading, Sandown and Lake. The **Isle of Wight Steam Railway** ① *T01983-882204, www.iwsteamrailway.co.uk*, connects with Island Line at Smallbrook Station. Rover Tickets can also be used on the Island line trains.

Tourist Information Isle of Wight Tourism ① *Osborne House Estate, York Av, East Cowes, T01983-813813, www.visitisleofwight.co.uk*. There is currently no walk-in information centre run by Isle of Wight Tourism on the island, however there is a Travel Centre at Ryde Bus Station run by **Southern Vectis** and good information at all the ferry terminals.

Northwest Wight → For listings, see pages 76-79.

The old harbour town of Yarmouth is the most attractive port of entry on the island. The pubs, restaurants and hotels gathered around its small town square can become impossibly busy in the summer, but out of season they make a very enjoyable day trip from the New Forest. A few miles east the marshland around the pretty little estuarine village of Newtown throngs with visiting birdlife. Almost bang in the middle of the island, Carisbrooke Castle on its little hill looks suitably noble and battered given its long history as a royal prison and Norman powerhouse. Next door, the island's capital on the River Medina at Newport is a sorry sight although it does have a beautiful guildhall, housing an informative local history museum. Directly due north, at the mouth of the Medina, Cowes has become synonymous with international yachting and all that very expensive sport entails.

Arriving in Northwest Wight
Getting there and around Ferries to Yarmouth run from Lymington and Keyhaven. Southern Vectis bus routes serve the Northwest Wight area, as well as the Island Coaster. → See Transport, page 79.

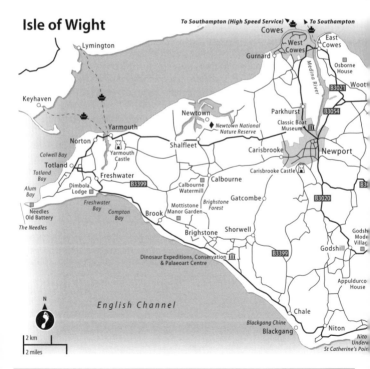

Yarmouth

Yarmouth is one of the most attractive towns on the island, its old harbour and town square yet to be overwhelmed by tourist tat, although it gets very crowded in the summer. Overlooking the harbour, **Yarmouth Castle** ① *(EH), T01983-760678, Apr-Oct Wed-Sun 1000-1600, £4, concessions £3.60, child (5-15) £2.40,* was Henry VIII's final coastal fortification, completed in the mid-16th century to protect the town from the French. It's an impressive building housing changing exhibitions of local painting and photos of old Yarmouth. The battlements afford fine views over the Solent; a good spot for picnics.

Newtown

About 5 miles east of Yarmouth, north of the main road to Newport, the tranquil little village of Newtown often wins the 'best-kept' award on the island, its cottage gardens a feast for the eyes in spring and summer. The strangely isolated little 17th-century brick and stone **Old Town Hall** ① *(NT), T01983-531785, mid-Mar to Oct Tue-Thu and Sun 1400-1700; Jul and Aug Mon-Thu, Sun 1400-1700, £3, under-16s £1.50,* is evidence that this was an important town in the Middle Ages. It became an infamous 'rotten borough', hugely over-represented in parliament, and done away with by the Reform Acts of the 1820s. Birdwatching and excellent coastal and marsh walks can be enjoyed in the **Newtown National Nature Reserve**.

Carisbrooke Castle

① *(EH), T01983-522107, www.carisbrooke castlemuseum.org.uk, Apr-Sep daily 1000-1800; Oct-Nov daily 1000-1600; Nov to mid-Feb Sat-Sun 1000-1600; check Feb-Mar opening times on website, £7.70, concessions £6.90, child (5-15) £4.60, family £20.*

The island's most important castle, at Carisbrooke, 5 miles further east on the A3054, commands tremendous panoramic views from its wall walk and remains surprisingly complete, its great stone walls and gatehouse standing proud at the top of a small hill. It started life as a Saxon camp, parts of which can still be seen below the Norman keep. The Redvers family ran the island from here until the death of Countess Isabella in 1293, when the castle was bought by Edward I, his son adding the great gatehouse. King Charles I was imprisoned here during the Civil War before his execution. The working donkey wheel deep well in the wethouse is the star attraction inside, along with an engaging museum with displays on island and castle life down the ages. Don't miss

the fabulous Princess Beatrice Garden based on a Privy Garden that existed in the early to mid-20th century.

Newport

Carisbrooke is on the outskirts of Newport, the capital of the island and not a particularly appealing sight. Surrounded by prisons, hospitals and ugly housing developments, the town's ancient origins have long been obscured. Even the Roman villa discovered here is best passed over for the one at Brading. In the centre stands John Nash's fine early 19th-century **guildhall**. The **Classic Boat Museum** ① *T01983-290006, www.classicboat museum.org, Apr-Oct daily 1000-1630, £4, concessions £3, child (5-16) £1*, in Newport Harbour, has a collection of vintage boats, including early dinghies and speed boats.

Cowes

Back on the coast, Cowes is the most renowned town on the island thanks to its global yachting associations. The home of the Royal Yacht Squadron, during **Cowes Week** (early August), and at boating events throughout the summer, the narrow old streets of Cowes are awash with yellow wellies, hearty boatowners, old seadogs and very focused professional yachties. The snob value of Cowes Week in the social calendar was confirmed when sailing became a royal hobby in the 19th century and shows no sign of diminishing, although the whole event has become significantly less amateurish. At any other time, the old town of West Cowes is an attractive and genteel place to poke around, connected to the more workaday East Cowes by the floating chain bridge (£2 per car).

Northeast Wight → *For listings, see pages 76-79.*

Queen Victoria's favourite summer retreat at Osborne House now draws in hordes of curious visitors. The opulence of its interior is unlikely to disappoint. Further west, Ryde is the other main ferry port, a Victorian town that has never quite achieved its grand aspirations. The more unassuming and quietly well-to-do seaside village of Seaview just along the coast is more of a magnet. Bembridge is another major yachting centre at the mouth of the River Yar. At Brading the Downs rise up to the south and the island's holiday spirit gets into gear.

Arriving in Northeast Wight

Getting there and around Ryde is the main ferry port on the eastern side of the island, but ferries also arrive at Cowes. The **Island Line** electric railway links Ryde with Smallbrook Junction, Brading, Sandown, Lake and Shanklin. The **Isle of Wight Steam Railway** runs from Smallbrook. The area is well served by **Southern Vectis** buses; see Transport, page 79.

Osbourne House

① *(EH), East Cowes, T01983-200022. Apr-Sep daily 1000-1800 (last admission 1600, house closes at 1700); Oct 1000-1700; Nov to mid-Feb Sat-Sun 1000-1600. £13.40, concessions £12.10, child (5-15) £8, family £34.80.*
A mile or so east of East Cowes, Osborne House is the single most visited place on the island, especially since featuring in the film *Mrs Brown*. Queen Victoria's 'little' holiday home, where she grieved well nigh inconsolably for her beloved Albert, is a pretty extraordinary Italianate

The Shipping Forecast

Broadcast four times a day on BBC Radio 4 Long Wave, shortly before 0500, 1200, 1800 and midnight, the shipping forecast has become almost as sacred an English institution as Trooping the Colour and cream teas. Heard for the first time in 1924, it uses a strange set of seemingly totemic names and mysterious coded shorthand to warn mariners of the weather conditions over the next 24 hours. The names pinpoint 30 sea areas. Some, such as Dover, Plymouth, Irish Sea and Hebrides, are self-explanatory and provide handy summaries of what it's likely to be like beside the seaside. The sound of others – Dogger, Bailey, Rockall, Sole, and Forties – brings the smack of the cold and briny open sea into cosy homes across the land. After the gale warnings and general synopsis, the forecast begins in the northeast with Viking, North and South Utsire, near Norway, and moves clockwise around the British Isles, through Tyne, Humber, Thames, Dover, Wight, Portland, Plymouth, and Lundy, and back up to the Faeroes, Fair Isle and southeast Iceland in the north again. Each sea area is followed by a three-part forecast describing the wind direction and strength on the Beaufort Scale, the weather expected, and the visibility: 'Cromarty, south-westerly backing southerly 4, increasing 5 or 6, occasionally 7. Rain spreading northeastwards. Moderate, becoming poor.' Controversy has recently surrounded the proposed replacement of the lullaby tune, *Sailing By*, that has introduced the midnight forecasts since 1965. Originally commissioned by the BBC to accompany an epic hot-air balloon ride over the Alps, its twee and lilting harmony would apparently be sorely missed by grizzled seafarers and snug landlubbers alike.

palace looking down on wide-terraced gardens and acres of rolling parkland. Designed by Thomas Cubitt (responsible for the look of Pimlico in London) around an old Georgian house in 1846, the inside is finished in an opulent style, full of marble, gilt, statuary and portraits of 19th-century European royalty. Also on show are the Queen's Dining Room, with place settings showing the 'order of precedence', and the Durbar Wing, where her youngest daughter Beatrice lived, including a magnificent room designed by Bhai Ram Singh in the 1890s to show off India, the jewel in Victoria's crown. An exhibition explains the lavish furnishings' contemporary relevance to the subcontinent today.

Ryde and Seaview

Ryde is the main ferry terminal on the east of the island but not somewhere many people would otherwise choose to visit. It has a certain amount of 'faded charm' but even in that department can't really beat the competition further south and west. Getting into the holiday spirit, though, old London tube trains take ferry passengers inland along the pier, depositing them at the bottom of Union Street. East of the Hoverport, the Esplanade might like to become the next Brighton, complete with its miniature oriental pavilion, but it clearly has some way to go. Anyone with transport is likely to do much better heading east for a couple of miles to **Seaview**, still a quiet little seaside village with a selection of good hotels, sandy beaches, warm breezes and views across the Solent of the twinkling orange lights of Portsmouth.

Bembridge

Next stop round the coast is Bembridge, popular with yachters, houseboat-dwellers and the retired. Half a mile south of Bembridge on the B3395 is the last surviving **windmill** ⓘ *(NT), High St, Bembridge, T01983-873945, mid-Mar to Nov, 1030-1700, £3.50, child £1.75,* on the island, built in the early 18th century with its wooden workings still intact.

Brading

From Bembridge a spectacular road heads over Culver Downs. Here is the well-sited but otherwise bog-standard pub, the **Culverhaven Inn**, as well as various gun emplacements, and good views overlooking Sandown and Shanklin. After 3 miles or so the road arrives in Brading, which provides a foretaste of the full-on appeal to the tourist purse made further along the coast. The remarkably good-value **Lilliput Antique Doll and Toy Museum** ⓘ *T01983-407231, www.lilliputmuseum.org.uk, daily 1000-1700, £2.50, under-14s £1.25,* is typical of the island in many ways: the museum's really impressive collection of old playthings is presented in a charming and amateurish way. Equally, the privately run **Roman Villa** ⓘ *T01983-406223, www.bradingromanvilla.org.uk, daily 0930-1700, £6.50, child (5-16) £3.75,* with its well-preserved hypocaust, intriguing and beautiful floor mosaics in a Roman room with a view crying out for a new roof, is much more accessible and enjoyable than many an overtended English Heritage site.

A mile northwards, a stiff walk past Morton Manor over Brading Down and through the Devil's Punch Bowl, stands **Nunwell House** ⓘ *T01983-407240, www.nunwellhouse.co.uk, 6-22 May, 3-26 Jun, 9-15 Sep Mon-Wed (call ahead as dates may change) 1000-1700, £6, under 16s £1.50,* a place with beautiful views and set in a garden designed by Vernon Russell-Smith. It's a fine-looking establishment where King Charles I spent his last night of freedom as a guest of the Oglander family, one of the oldest on the island, who still look after the place today.

Southeast Wight → *For listings, see pages 76-79.*

The island's reputation for seaside holiday heaven (or hell) emanates from the resorts of Sandown and Shanklin: amusement arcade wonderlands with a tacky style all their own that people tend to either love or loathe. Round the corner, Bonchurch is quietly superior to their boisterous charms, tucked into the peculiar geological landslip bursting with exotic vegetation known as the Undercliff. Next door, Ventnor is a solidly picturesque seaside town tumbling down to a little sandy bay. A short hop inland, Godshill draws in the crowds to wonder at its picture-postcard setting, model village and remarkable church.

Sandown and Shanklin

Two miles south of Brading, the wide sweep of Sandown Bay is almost entirely taken up with the twin resorts of **Sandown** and **Shanklin**. These two fulfill most people's ready image of the 'holiday island', with their esplanades, sandy beaches, crumbling hotels and relentless tacky amusements. Sandown is marginally more geriatric, while Shanklin boasts the thatched, illuminated (May-September) and awesomely twee **Shanklin Chine** ⓘ *T01983-866432, www.shanklinchine.co.uk, Apr-Oct daily 1000-dusk, £4, child (5-14) £2.20,* a ravine running down the cliff full of rare plants and used as a training ground for commandos during the war. Henry 'Hiawatha' Longfellow visited it in 1868, leaving some verses on the drinking fountain near the top of the chine.

If you're visiting with kids, **Dinosaur Isle** ① *Culver Parade, Sandown, T01983-404344, www.dinosaurisle.com, Apr-Sep 1000-1800, Oct 1000-1700, Nov-Mar 1000-1600, £5, child (3-15) £3.70,* is well worth a visit to explore the prehistoric significance of the Isle of Wight. Visitors can also book fossil walks and guided horse rides.

Bonchurch and Ventnor

Round the corner beyond Dunnose, 3 miles along the pretty Undercliff, the closest the Isle of Wight comes to a corniche road, Bonchurch and Ventnor are a much more solidly attractive south-facing mix of seaside amusements, good restaurants and reasonable accommodation. All of which contributes effectively to a happy holiday mood, nestling below St Boniface Down. The aesthetic poet Algernon Swinburne lived in a house called East Dene in Bonchurch as a boy and played with Dickens' sons when the novelist stopped over in 1849, but he found the air distasteful and left for breezy Broadstairs in Kent.

The **Ventnor Botanic Garden** ① *T01983-855397, www.botanic.co.uk, Apr-Oct 1000-dusk, £5, child (6-16) £3, family £12,* features several acres of exotic plants from Australasia, South Africa and Mexico, as well as a herb garden and banana trees. On the coast near the gardens is the bijou **Steephill Cove**, a tiny cove that's packed in summer as it's such a special little beach with a shabby chic shops selling stylish nautical bits 'n' bobs, plus some wonderful cafés.

Three miles north of the botanic gardens along the B3327, a narrow track leads off to the left and a striking ruined stately home set in Capability Brown-landscaped gardens. **Appledurcombe House** ① *Wroxall, T01983-852484, www.appuldurcombe.co.uk, Apr-Oct, Sun-Fri 1000-1600, £2, under-16s £1.50, concessions £2.25,* was once the grandest on the island but fell prey to some strange adulterous shenanigans amongst its owners, an amusing story told on information boards in the empty shell. Now its austere Palladian architecture stands lonely and elegant in its gardens, crying out to be sketched. The grounds are a beautiful spot for a picnic and there's a falconry centre next door.

Godshill

As if the Chine were not enough, Godshill, 5 miles west of Shanklin on the A3020, must rank as one of the most ridiculously quaint little villages in England. Its unusual double-naved church claims to be among the top 10 'most visited' in the country, perhaps to see the wonderful Lily Crucifix mural from 1440 – painted over during the Reformation and uncovered in the 19th century – but also no doubt to ask forgiveness for the huge cream teas taken in the village. Almost inevitably, in the gardens of the old vicarage, there's a **model village** ① *T01983-840270, www.modelvillagegodshill.co.uk, Mar-Sep 1000-1700, £3.95, child (3-16) £2.95, concessions £3.50,* a good example of its type, with tiny people enjoying a very hearty variety of outdoor activities dotted about between 1:10-scale stone houses with miniaturized gardens and a 1:20-scale model railway. The other attraction, the **Shell Museum**, with a collection of fossils, shells and minerals, is almost overwhelmed by its gift shop.

South and west Wight → *For listings, see pages 76-79.*

The least over-developed and most scenic part of the island, the southern coast path around St Catherine's Point, St Catherine's Hill and the downs above Brighstone provide the best walking country. Along with a few less busy old villages like Shorwell and Calbourne, the southwest is also home to several good-quality visitor attractions such as the gardens at Mottistone Manor, the Dinosaur Farm Museum, the working watermill at Calbourne and Dimbola Lodge, the former home of pioneer portrait photographer Julia Cameron. To the west, the island peters out beyond Freshwater in dramatic style with the sea-swept chalk stacks of the Needles.

St Catherine's Point

Six miles west along the coastal A3055 from Ventnor, St Catherine's Point is the most southerly headland on the island. It's a lovely cliffside spot with a little lighthouse overlooked by St Catherine's Hill, the highest point on the island (by 1 m over St Boniface Down to the east). On the summit, a medieval lighthouse, known as the Pepperpot but officially named **St Catherine's Oratory**, stands next to the **Saltcellar**, an abortive 19th-century attempt at a lighthouse (because of the frequent fog), used as a gun emplacement during the Second World War. On the road at the foot of the hill, close to the UK's oldest theme park, **Blackgang Chine Amusement Park**, there's a strange little **Temple to Shakespeare**, a shrine quoting verses from the *Two Gentlemen of Verona* put up by Thomas Letts, of diary fame.

The A3055 runs northwest along the coast, a military road constructed to repel French invaders, after six miles passing the **Dinosaur Expeditions, Conservation and Palaeoart Centre** ⓘ *T01983-740844, www.dinosaurexpeditions.co.uk, £5, under-16s £2.50*. Established following the discovery of a well-preserved brachiosaurus in 1992, it's where fossils found on hunts can be identified and rare specimens can be seen in the process of conservation by experts.

Shorwell and Brighstone

At Chale, the B3399 heads north inland to the picturesque village of **Shorwell**, an excellent base for walks on the central downland. **Limerstone Down**, 2 miles west of the village, provides particularly wide-reaching views of almost the entire sea-girt little island. At the foot of the hill is another sweet village, **Brighstone**, with an interesting village museum in a row of cute thatched cottages with a National Trust shop. The Trust's most impressive property on the island is 2 miles west of Brighstone, at **Mottistone Manor** ⓘ *(NT), T01983-741302, garden open Mar-Oct, Mon-Thu, Sun, 1100-1700, £4.15, child £2.05*, the place to take in sea views, teas and some colourful herbaceous borders in a 16th-century manor house garden.

Heading inland, north of Mottistone, is **Brighstone Forest**. The National Trust car park here is where the Tennyson Trail through beautiful hillside beech woods and along the ridge of the downs can be followed west to the Needles about eight miles away. Through the forest, at **Calbourne**, there's a working **watermill** ⓘ *T01983-531227, www.calbourne watermill.co.uk, Apr-Oct daily 1000-1700, £7, concessions £6, child (5-16) £4*, with grinding demonstrations daily at 1500. It's surrounded by quirky museums and there's punting on the mill pond and a bouncy galleon for kids. There's a good café selling cakes and bread using home-ground flour.

Freshwater Bay and The Needles
Back on the south coast, at Freshwater Bay, five miles west of Mottistone, the large seaside house called **Dimbola Lodge** ① *Terrace Lane, Freshwater Bay, T01983-756814, www.dimbola.co.uk, Apr-Oct daily 1000-1700, Nov-Mar Tue-Sun 1000-1600, £4, under-16s free*, is where the pioneer photographer Julia Cameron lived and worked. It has been preserved, with a permanent exhibition of her Victorian portraits 'Famous Men and Fair Women' and also changing shows on contemporary photographers. There's an excellent vegetarian restaurant with sea views as well as workshops and other events.

The walk from Brighstone continues west along Compton Down affording magnificent sea views southwards. To the south below is **Compton Bay**, famous for its very clean beaches. The chalk ridge continues along **Tennyson Down** and **High Down**, ending up at **The Needles** in the west. It's worth checking out the **Old Battery** ① *(NT), West Highdown, Totland, T01983-741020, Mar-Oct, Tue, Thu, Sat-Sun, 1030-1700, £4.80, child £2.40, family £12*, built into the cliffs here, alongside a strange rocket testing site. The fort was built in 1862 to protect against the threat of French invasion, with a 200-ft tunnel leading to spectacular views of the Hampshire and Dorset coast. Its gun barrels are still in place, and the searchlight position is accessible up winding a spiral staircase. The 1940s tearoom is a treat.

Isle of Wight listings

For hotel and restaurant price codes, and other relevant information, see pages 9-12.

Northwest Wight *p68*

£££ The George Hotel, Yarmouth, T01983-760331, www.thegeorge.co.uk. One of the best hotels on the island, run by the same people as the **Master Builder's House Hotel** in Buckler's Hard, New Forest (see page 63). Very good airy brasserie with outdoor seating next to a rather stuffy smart restaurant.

££ Duke of York, Mill Hill Rd, Cowes, T01983-295171, www.dukeofyorkcowes.co.uk. A very lively and friendly old pub just up from the floating bridge. Expect the whole town to be booked solid in the summer.

££ Jireh House, St James Sq, Yarmouth T01983-760513, www.jireh-house.com. A 17th-century house with a cosy restaurant and rooms.

Northeast Wight *p70*

£££ Northbank Hotel, Seaview, T01983-612227, www.northbankhotel.co.uk. Pleasant 18-room family-run Victorian hotel right on the beach in the middle of the village boasting an Aga-cooked menu.

£££ Priory Bay Hotel, Priory Dr, Seaview, T01983-613146, www.priorybay.co.uk. Perhaps the classiest hotel on the island, on the site of an old priory with converted barns, gardens and a highly rated restaurant. Now offers luxury designer yurts in the grounds.

£££ Seaview Hotel, High St, Seaview, T01983-612711, www.seaviewhotel.co.uk. Popular restaurant and comfortable hotel in the centre of the village, both acclaimed by the national press, something of a haven for the more affluent Seaviewers.

£££ Springvale Hotel, Seaview, T01983-812905. This beautifully positioned Edwardian house overlooking the Solent makes an eccentric alternative to staying in the village.

£££ Vintage Vacations, T07802-758113, www.vintagevacations.co.uk. Offers a range of alternative accommodation including vintage airstream trailers, converted scouts hut and now **The Meadow**, a low-cost fun camping option, all with a 1950s vibe.

££ Crab and Lobster Inn, 32 Foreland Fields Rd, Bembridge, T01983-872244, www.crabandlobsterinn.co.uk. Busy pub with rooms in a fine position on the most eastern tip of the island. Local seafood is a speciality, but parking in summer can be impossible.

££ Little Upton Farm, Gatehouse Rd, Ashey, T01983-563236, www.littleupton farm.co.uk. A working farm on the outskirts of Ryde, close to the Steam railway stop at Ashey.

££ Newham Farm, Binstead, Rude, T01983-882423, www.newhamfarm.co.uk. 17th-century working farm built on the site of an abbey. Easy-going, friendly atmosphere, impeccable service and magnificent breakfasts. A real find. Highly recommended.

Southeast Wight *p72*

££££ The Hambrough, Ventnor, T01983-856333, www.robert-thompson.com. Designer rooms by the sea with everything from Illy Espresso Machine to underfloor heating. Definitely the design end of what the Isle of Wight has to offer. The restaurant at **The Hambrough** is headed up by Robert Thompson, a Michelin-star chef.

£££ Luccombe Manor Country House Hotel, Popham Rd, Shanklin, T01983-869000, www.luccombemanor.co.uk. Elegant hotel with beautiful views.

£££ Royal Hotel, Belgrave Rd, Ventnor, T01983-852186, www.royalhoteliow.co.uk. The grandest hotel in Ventnor, elegant, restrained and airy, with heated outdoor pool and sea views.

££ Hillside Hotel, Mitchell Av, Ventnor, T01983-852271, www.hillsideventnor.co.uk.

Charming 18th-century house-turned-hotel overlooking Ventnor from the foot of Boniface Down. Extensively refurbished with refreshing contemporary Scandinavian interiors and good bistro and stables.

££ Spyglass Inn, Esplanade, Ventnor, T01983-855338, www.thespyglass.com. Small rooms with sea views above a very convivial pub (see below).

Self-catering
Nettlecombe Farm, Whitwell, T01983-730783, www.nettlecombefarm.co.uk. This working farm offers luxury self-catering in converted farm buildings, coarse fishing and yoga retreats.

South and west Wight *p74*
£££ Swainston Manor Hotel, Calbourne, T01983-521121, www.swainstonmanor.co.uk. Grand old country house in a beautiful garden with old-fashioned, slightly run-down furnishings.

££ North Court, Shorwell, T01983-740415, www.northcourt.info. Jacobean mansion set in 14 acres of carefully tended gardens. There's a snooker table in the library, croquet and lawn tennis. No smoking.

££ Rockstone Cottage, Colwell Chine Rd, near **Totland**, T01983-753723, www.rockstonecottage.co.uk. Stylish B&B with attractive garden.

££ Westcourt Farm, Shorwell, T01983-740233, www.westcourt-farm.co.uk. Charming old Elizabethan manor house with beautiful views and cosy rooms. No smoking.

£ Totland Bay YHA, Hurst Hill, Totland Bay, T0845-3719348, www.yha.org.uk/hostel/totland. Best budget option near the Needles.

🍴 Restaurants

Northwest Wight *p68*
££ The Gossips Café, The Square, Yarmouth, T01983-760646, www.the gossipscafe.co.uk. Lively and welcoming café with a cool 1950s vibe and views across the Solent. Hearty food

and fabulous Minghella ice cream. Free Wi-Fi too.

££ Café Mozart, 48 High St, Cowes, T01983-293681. Offers Frenchified light meals with main courses costing about £10.

££ The New Inn, Mill Rd, Shalfleet, T01983-531314, www.thenew-inn.co.uk. A pub with a riverside garden serving food of a high standard. Has earned a reputation for its excellent fish dishes.

££ Salty's, Quay St, Yarmouth, T01983-761550. A harbourside restaurant patronized by the locals, who come for the fish and busy downstairs bar, one of the most highly rated places on the island.

££ Valentino's, 93 High St, Carisbrooke, T01983-522458. A mid-range Italian restaurant popular with the locals.

£ Murray's The Seafood Restaurant, 106 High St, Cowes, T01983-296233, www.murrays.co. Has a long-standing reputation for its fresh fish and seafood.

£ Primefood Delicatessan, 62 High St, Cowes, T01983-291111, www.prime food.co.uk. A superior deli and a good place to pick up provisions for your boat or put together a picnic.

£ Yorkies Fish and Chips, 55 High St, Cowes, T01983-291713. A famous old-fashioned chippy.

Northeast Wight *p70*
££ Baywatch on the Beach, The Duver, St Helens, T01983-873259. Right by the beach, this restaurant is nautical and friendly by day, come evening, the tea lights are on and it's a relaxing restaurant for couples and families with everything from burgers to seafood.

££ Ivar Cottage, Hillway, Bembridge, T01983-885040, www.ivarcottagesummerhouse.co.uk. Sweet little cottage garden on the B3395, 4 miles west of Bembridge, where absolutely fresh crab and lobster can be enjoyed or taken away for a picnic. Also a B&B.

££ The Net, Sherborne St, Bembridge, T01983-875800. A newish style restaurant that's a winner with the sailing fraternity. There's a brasserie menu and regularly changing fusion food dinner menu.

££ The Old Fort, Esplanade, Seaview, T01983-612363, www.oldfortbarcafe.co.uk. A strange combination of diner and bar. This social hub right on the seafront offers competent cuisine.

Southeast Wight *p72*

£££ The Hambrough, Ventnor, T01983-856333, www.robert-thompson.com/restaurants. Fine dining by Michelin-star chef, Robert Thompson.

££ Bonchurch Inn, The Shute, Bonchurch, T01983-852611, www.bonchurch-inn.co.uk. Italian food and English staples in a curio-crammed olde-worlde pub in a very pretty village.

££ The Pond Café, Bonchurch, T01983-855666, www.robert-thompson.com/restaurants. Relaxed and reliably good all-day dining and Sun lunches from the same owner as **The Hambrough**.

££ Spyglass Inn, Esplanade, Ventnor, T01983-855338, www.thespyglass.com. South-facing and right beside the sea, very popular with families (also does rooms) and doing reasonably good food that can be enjoyed outside braving the gulls and spume at high tide.

South and west Wight *p74*

££ Edulis (meaning 'edible plant'), Ventnor Botanic Gardens, T01983-855397, www.botanic.co.uk. Newly opened café and restaurant with picture windows onto the Mediterranean garden, serving ultra-fresh cuisine with fine local produce. The 'Half Hour' salad has ingredients picked on site and on the plate within half an hour.

££ The Red Lion, Church Pl, Freshwater, T01983-754925, www.redlion-freshwater.co.uk. Quiet but very popular pub doing an above-average menu prepared from fresh ingredients, in one of the more attractive corners of Freshwater, up by the old church. Recommended.

££ The Waterfront Restaurant, Totland, T01983-756969, www.thewaterfront-iow.co.uk. Great position on the beach, with stunning sunset views. The food and ambience are average.

££-£ Wheelers Crab Shed, Steephill Cove, T01983-852177, www.steephillcove-isleofwight.co.uk. Popular shack-cum-beach café where Mandy Wheeler sells her legendary crab sandwiches and lobster salads. Highly recommended.

£ The Buddle Inn, St Catherine's Rd, Niton Undercliff, T01983-730243, www.buddle inn.co.uk. Attractive old pub with a large garden and model of Carisbrooke Castle out front, near the south coast path, doing reliable and reasonably priced pub grub.

£ Gatcombe Tearooms, Little Gatcombe Farm, Newbarn Lane, Gatcombe, T01983-721580, www.littlegatcombefarm.co.uk. Sidney the peacock patrols outside this modern farmhouse where good home-made teas can be taken just beneath the downs in the middle of the island. Also a B&B.

❀ Festivals

Jun Isle of Wight Festival, www.isleofwight festival.com. Music festival taking place in Seaclose Park near Newport.
Aug Cowes Week, www.cowesweek.co.uk. Sailing regatta with up to 1000 boats.
Sep Bestival, www.bestival.net. 4-day music festival held in Robin Hill Country Park, www.robin-hill.com.

⛰ What to do

Northwest Wight *p68*
Boating
Ocean Blue Sea Charters, Eastern Esplanade, Ventnor, T01983-852398, www.oceanblueseacharters.co.uk. Join the 'Cheetah' catamaran and explore the

spectacular Undercliff Coastline or take a
lobster safari.

Climbing
Goodleaf Tree Climbing, Seaview, T0333-
8001188, www.goodleaf.co.uk. Aboreal
adventures in the trees for all the family.

Horse riding
Brickfields, Newnham Rd, Binstead, near
Ryde, T01983-566801, www.brickfields.net.
Daily all year 1000-1700. Also has pigs, rare
breeds, a tractor museum and special events.
Romany Riding Stables, on a minor road to
the north off the A3054, 3 miles west of
Newport, signposted Little Whitehouse,
T01983-525467, www.epony.co.uk. Offers
very good-value riding lessons and hacking
in a welcoming if rather scruffy yard.

⊖ Transport

Bus The following services are the
Southern Vectis routes connecting the
main island towns. For further details
see www.islandbuses.info.
Route 1 Newport–St Mary's
Hospital–Parkhurst–Northwood–Cowes
Route 2 Newport–Merstone–Godshill–
Shanklin–Sandown–Brading–Tesco–Ryde
Route 3 Newport–Godshill-Wroxall–
Ventnor–Shanklin–Sandown–Tesco–Ryde
Route 4 East Cowes–Osborne House–
Whippingham–Wootton–Binstead–Ryde
Route 5 Newport–Whippingham–
Osborne–East Cowes
Route 6 Newport–Chale–Blackgang Chine–
Niton–Whitwell/St Lawrence–Ventnor
Route 7 Newport–Shalfleet–Cranmore/
Wellow–Yarmouth–Freshwater–Totland–
Alum Bay
Route 8 Newport–Arreton–Sandown–
Bembridge–Seaview–Ryde
Route 9 Newport–Fairlee/Staplers–
Wootton–Binstead–Ryde

Route 12 Newport–Brighstone–Freshwater
Bay–Totland
Route 37 Ryde–Binstead–Haylands–Ryde
Route 38 Newport–Gunville–Carisbrooke–
Whitepit Lane–Newport

Northwest Wight *p68*
Bicycle
Wight Cycle Hire, Yarmouth, T01983-
761800, www.wightcyclehire.co.uk;
Wight Mountain, Newport, T01983-533445,
www.wightmountain.com.

Car
Ford Rental, River Way, Newport, T01983-
245050, www.premierfordrental.co.uk;
Solent Self Drive Ltd, 32 High St, Cowes,
T01983-299056, www.isleofwighthire.co.uk.

Northeast Wight *p70*
Bicycle
Battersby Cycles, Ryde, T01983-562039;
Bikemech, Freshwater, T01983-756787;
P Rentals, Benbridge, T0800-9173494;
Isle of Wight Cycle Hire, Sandown,
T01983-4000055; **Offshore Sports**,
Shanklin, T01983-866269.

Car
Bartletts Service Station, 5 Langbridge,
Newchurch, Sandown, T01983-865338,
www.bartlettsservicestation.co.uk; **Hillstone
Self Drive Car Hire**, Osborne Rd, Shanklin,
T01983-864263.

⊙ Directory

**Hospitals Isle of Wight NHS Primary Care
Trust, St Mary's Hospital**, Parkhurst Rd,
Newport, T01983-524081, www.iow.nhs.uk.
The Orchard Hospital,189 Fairlee Rd,
Newport, T01983-520022, www.private
healthcare.co.uk. **Library** East Cowes
Library, York Centre, York Av, East Cowes,
T01983-293019.

Contents

82   Index

Footnotes

Index

A

Abbotsbury 30
accommodation 9
    price codes 10
Affpuddle 24
air travel 6
airport information 6-7
Alum Chine 26
Alvediston 47
Andover 54
Appledurcombe House 73
art galleries 16
Askerswell 35
Athelhampton 24
ATMs 13

B

Badbury Rings 22
banks 13
beach huts 26
Beaminster 31
Beaulieu 60
beer 12
Bembridge 72
bicycle 9
Bishops Waltham 55
bitter 12
Blandford Forum 21
Bolderwood Green 60
Bonchurch 73
Bournemouth 24
    beaches 26
    listings 32
    Oceanarium 26
    Russell-Cotes Art Gallery 26
Bovington Tank Museum 29
Brading 72
Branksome Chine 26
Breamore 44
Breamore Manor 44
Bridport 31
Brighstone 74
Brighstone Forest 74
Brownsea Island 26
Buckler's Hard 60
bus travel 8

C

Calbourne 74
camping 11
car hire 9
car travel 8

Carisbrooke Castle 69
cash point machines 13
Cerne Abbas 24
Chalbury 22
Charmouth 33
Chettle House 20
Christchurch 62
cider 12
Clearbury Ring 44
climate 6
Clouds Hill 29
coach travel 8
Compton Chamberlayne 45
Corfe Castle 27
cost of travelling 14
Cowes 70
Cowes Week 70
Cranborne Chase 20
Cranborne Manor 22
credit cards 13
crop circle 43
currency cards 14
cycling 9

D

Damerham 63
Danebury 54
Danebury Hill Fort 54
Danebury Vineyard 54
Dinosaur Expeditions,
    Conservation and Palaeoart
    Centre 74
Dinosaur Isle 73
Dinton Park 45
disabled travellers 13
Dorchester 23
Dorset 18
Dorset Downs 21
drink 12
Druids 41
Durdle Door 29
Durlston Head 28

E

East Lulworth 29
Eggardon Hill 31
electricity 13
emergency services 13
English Heritage (EH) 16
English Nature 16
Evershot 32, 34

F

Fawley 65
ferries, Isle of Wight 67
Fiddleford Manor 20
Flaghead 26
food 12
Fordingbridge 62
Fovant Badges 45
Freshwater Bay 75
Fyfield Bavant 45

G

Gillingham 32
Godshill 73
guesthouses 9

H

Hardy, Thomas 24
health 13
Higher Brockhampton 24
Hindon 32
Hinton Ampner 55
Hospital of St Cross 53
hospitals 13
hostels 9
hotels 9
    price codes 10
Hurst Castle 61

I

Ibberton 34
INTECH Science Centre 53
Isle of Purbeck 27
Isle of Wight 66
    listings 76

J

Jurassic Coast 29

K

Keyhaven 61
Kimmeridge 28
King's Barrow Down 44
Kingston Lacy 22
Knowlton 22

L

Larmer Tree Gardens 20
Lawrence, TE 29
London City Airport 7
Lower Bockhampton 32

Lulworth Castle 29
Lulworth Cove 28
Lyme 31
Lyme Regis 29, 31, 33
Lymington 61
Lyndhurst 59

M

Maiden Castle 24
Mapperton Gardens 31
Marwell Zoological Park 55
Meon Valley 55
Milford-on-Sea 62
Millyford Bridge 60
Milton Abbas 23
Milton Abbey 23
Monarch's Way 44
money 13
money transfers 14
Moreton 34
Mottisfont Abbey 54
Mottistone Manor 74
museums 16

N

National Motor Museum 60
National Trust (NT) 16
Needles, the 75
New Alresford 55
New Forest 58
    listings 63
    walks 60
New Forest Wildlife Park 59
New Milton 63
Newport 70
Newtown 69
Nunton 47
Nunwell House 72

O

Ober Corner 60
Old Wardour Castle 20
Old Winchester Hill 55
Opening hours 14
Osbourne House 70
Overstrand 26

P

Philipps House 45
Poole 26
    listings 32
Portland Bill 30
post 14
Poundsbury 23
Powerstock 35
price codes 10

eating 10
sleeping 10
Priors Dean 57
pubs 12

R

restaurants 12
    price codes 10
Ringwood 62
Rockbourne Roman Villa 62
Romsey 54
Romsey Abbey 54
Royal Signals Museum 22
Ryde 71

S

safety 15
Salisbury 38
    Cathedral 42
    listings 46
    Market Square 40
    Mompesson House 41
    The Wardrobe 41
Salisbury Plain 44
Sandbanks 26
Sandown 72
Seacombe 28
Seaview 71
Selborne 55
Semley 32
Shaftesbury 19
    listings 32
Shanklin 72
Shanklin Chine 72
Sherborne 19
    listings 32
Sherborne Abbey 20
Shipping Forecast 71
Shorwell 74
Solent Way 61
St Alban's Head 28
St Aldhelm's Head 28
St Catherine's Point 74
St Cross Hospital 53
Steep 57
Steephill Cove 73
Stockbridge 54,56
Stonehenge 43
Sturminster Newton 20
Swanage 28
Swanage Steam Railway 27

T

taxes 14
Teffont Evias 46
Teffont Magna 45

telephone 15
Test Valley 54
Test Way 54
time zone 15
tipping 15
Tolpuddle Martyrs 29
train 8
transport 6
    air 6
    bus 8
    coach 8
    train 8
Trent 34
Tyneham 28

U

Upham 57

V

Value Added Tax 14
Ventnor 73
Ventnor Botanic Garden 73
visas 16

W

Wareham 27,33
West Bay 31
West Bexington 33
Weymouth 29
    Portland Bill 30
    Sea Life Adventure Park 30
when to go 6
White, Gilbert 55
Wilton House 44
Wimborne Minster 22
Wimborne Model Town 22
Winchester 48
    cathedral 52
    City Museum 52
    Hospital of St Cross 53
    listings 56
    Peninsula Barracks 51
    Westgate and Great Hall 51
Winspit 28
Woodfords, the 44
Worbarrow Tout 28
Worth Matravers 28
Wylye 46

Y

Yarmouth 69
Yarmouth Castle 69
youth hostels 10

Notes

Notes

Notes

Notes

Titles available in the Footprint *Focus* range

Latin America	UK RRP	US RRP
Bahia & Salvador	£7.99	$11.95
Brazilian Amazon	£7.99	$11.95
Brazilian Pantanal	£6.99	$9.95
Buenos Aires & Pampas	£7.99	$11.95
Cartagena & Caribbean Coast	£7.99	$11.95
Costa Rica	£8.99	$12.95
Cuzco, La Paz & Lake Titicaca	£8.99	$12.95
El Salvador	£5.99	$8.95
Guadalajara & Pacific Coast	£6.99	$9.95
Guatemala	£8.99	$12.95
Guyana, Guyane & Suriname	£5.99	$8.95
Havana	£6.99	$9.95
Honduras	£7.99	$11.95
Nicaragua	£7.99	$11.95
Northeast Argentina & Uruguay	£8.99	$12.95
Paraguay	£5.99	$8.95
Quito & Galápagos Islands	£7.99	$11.95
Recife & Northeast Brazil	£7.99	$11.95
Rio de Janeiro	£8.99	$12.95
São Paulo	£5.99	$8.95
Uruguay	£6.99	$9.95
Venezuela	£8.99	$12.95
Yucatán Peninsula	£6.99	$9.95

Asia	UK RRP	US RRP
Angkor Wat	£5.99	$8.95
Bali & Lombok	£8.99	$12.95
Chennai & Tamil Nadu	£8.99	$12.95
Chiang Mai & Northern Thailand	£7.99	$11.95
Goa	£6.99	$9.95
Gulf of Thailand	£8.99	$12.95
Hanoi & Northern Vietnam	£8.99	$12.95
Ho Chi Minh City & Mekong Delta	£7.99	$11.95
Java	£7.99	$11.95
Kerala	£7.99	$11.95
Kolkata & West Bengal	£5.99	$8.95
Mumbai & Gujarat	£8.99	$12.95

Africa & Middle East	UK RRP	US RRP
Beirut	£6.99	$9.95
Cairo & Nile Delta	£8.99	$12.95
Damascus	£5.99	$8.95
Durban & KwaZulu Natal	£8.99	$12.95
Fès & Northern Morocco	£8.99	$12.95
Jerusalem	£8.99	$12.95
Johannesburg & Kruger National Park	£7.99	$11.95
Kenya's Beaches	£8.99	$12.95
Kilimanjaro & Northern Tanzania	£8.99	$12.95
Luxor to Aswan	£8.99	$12.95
Nairobi & Rift Valley	£7.99	$11.95
Red Sea & Sinai	£7.99	$11.95
Zanzibar & Pemba	£7.99	$11.95

Europe	UK RRP	US RRP
Bilbao & Basque Region	£6.99	$9.95
Brittany West Coast	£7.99	$11.95
Cádiz & Costa de la Luz	£6.99	$9.95
Granada & Sierra Nevada	£6.99	$9.95
Languedoc: Carcassonne to Montpellier	£7.99	$11.95
Málaga	£5.99	$8.95
Marseille & Western Provence	£7.99	$11.95
Orkney & Shetland Islands	£5.99	$8.95
Santander & Picos de Europa	£7.99	$11.95
Sardinia: Alghero & the North	£7.99	$11.95
Sardinia: Cagliari & the South	£7.99	$11.95
Seville	£5.99	$8.95
Sicily: Palermo & the Northwest	£7.99	$11.95
Sicily: Catania & the Southeast	£7.99	$11.95
Siena & Southern Tuscany	£7.99	$11.95
Sorrento, Capri & Amalfi Coast	£6.99	$9.95
Skye & Outer Hebrides	£6.99	$9.95
Verona & Lake Garda	£7.99	$11.95

North America	UK RRP	US RRP
Vancouver & Rockies	£8.99	$12.95

Australasia	UK RRP	US RRP
Brisbane & Queensland	£8.99	$12.95
Perth	£7.99	$11.95

For the latest books, e-books and a wealth of travel information, visit us at:
www.footprinttravelguides.com.

footprinttravelguides.com

Join us on facebook for the latest travel news, product releases, offers and amazing competitions:
www.facebook.com/footprintbooks.